Old Amble and Warkworth

Guthrie Hutton

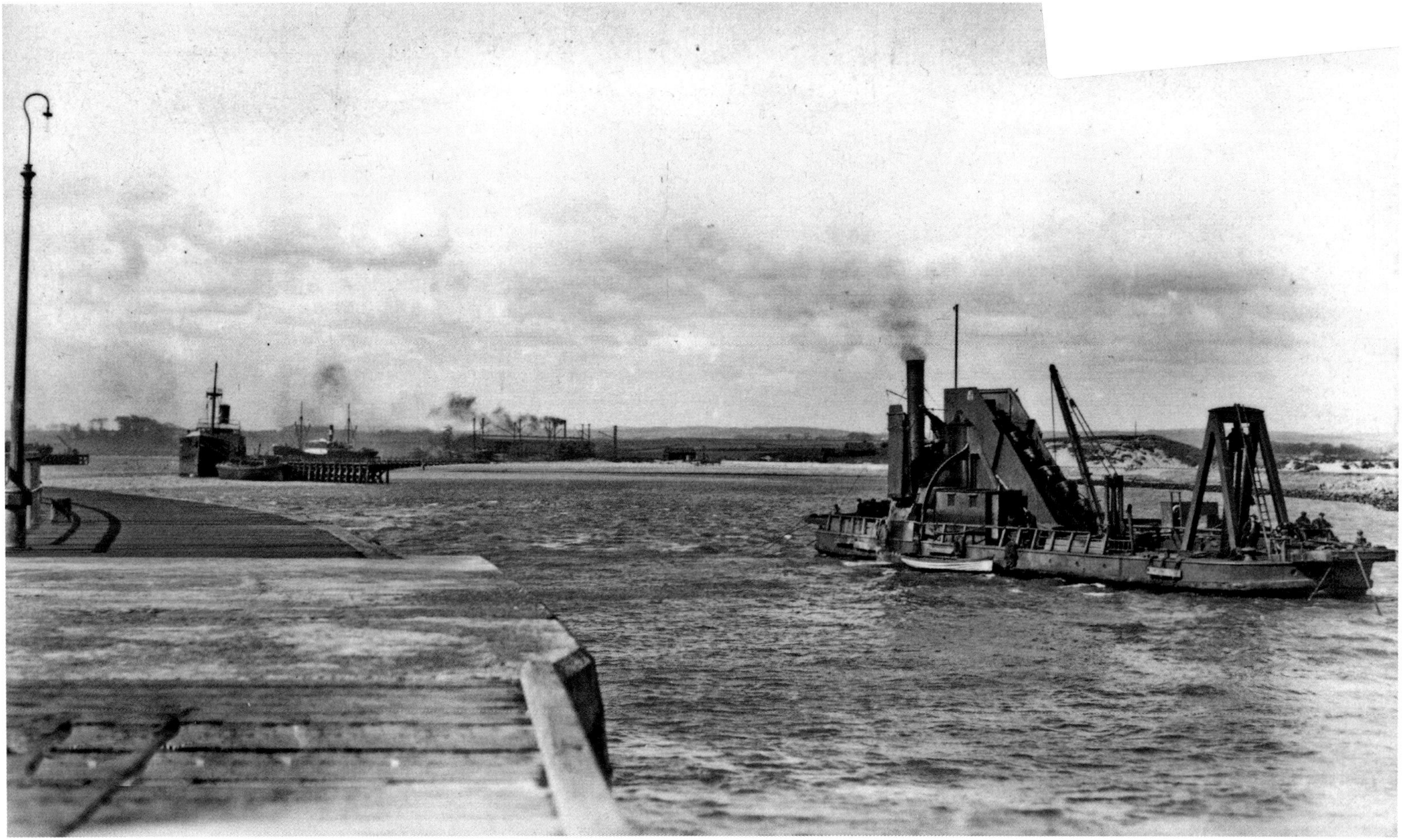

Clearing the silt in the harbour and especially the bar at the harbour mouth kept dredgers like the Hugh Andrews busy. She was built at Paisley on the River Cart, a tributary of the Clyde, in 1893 by the specialist firm, Fleming and Ferguson.

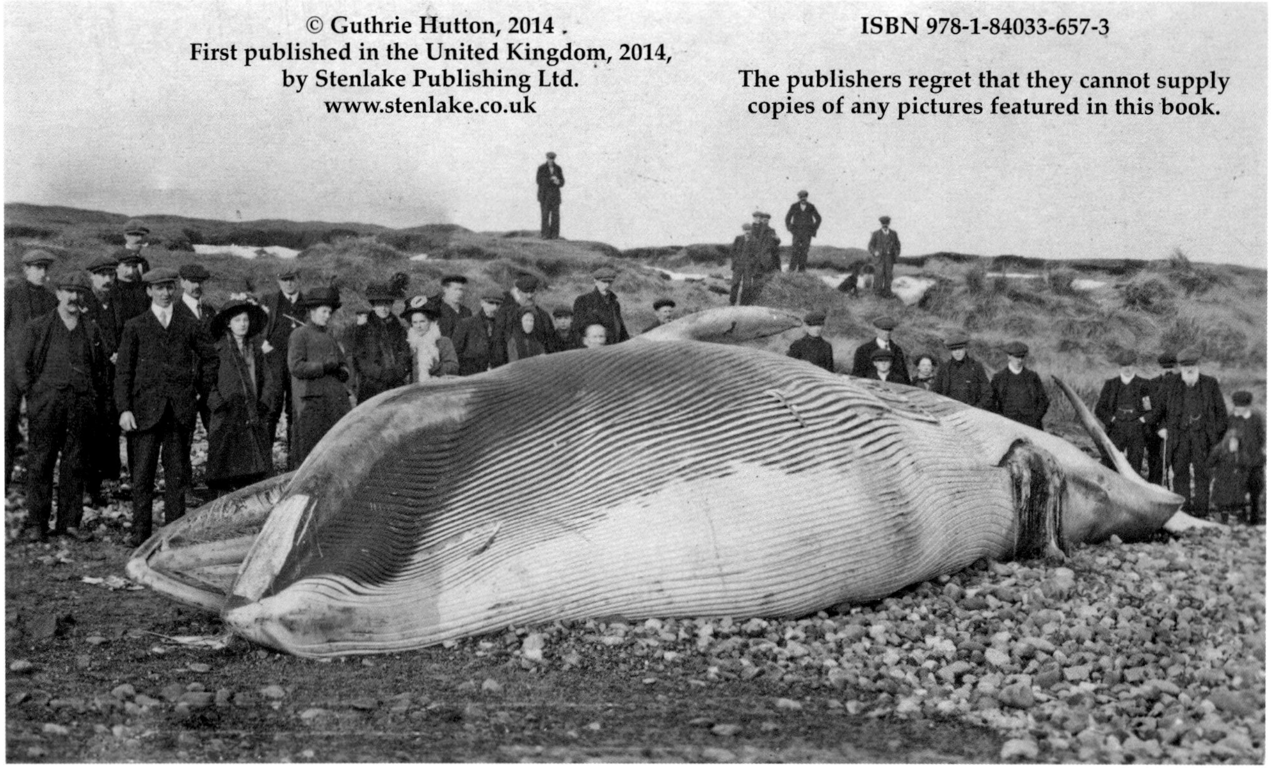

When whales get stranded they attract a lot of attention, as this beast on the beach at Hauxley has done. Another whale was apparently washed ashore at Hauxley in the 1770s and there have been many other whales, of various species, beached on the Northumberland coast over the centuries.

First published in the United Kingdom, 2014,
by Stenlake Publishing Ltd.
www.stenlake.co.uk

ISBN 978-1-84033-657-3

Acknowledgements

It would have been impossible to compile this little book without the help of George Nairn. I must therefore thank him for his splendid contribution, and for the kindly and generous way that he made this happen. I must also thank the friendly and helpful staff at Amble and Alnwick libraries. Thanks are due too to the often anonymous compilers of web sites – too numerous to list – that I consulted in the course of writing the stories that accompany some of the pictures in the book. Much of the information on the story of the *Ina Mactavish* came from an excellent article in Picture Postcard Annual 2008, written by Alan Leonard.

Further Reading

The books listed below were used by the author during his research. None are available from Stenlake Publishing; please contact your local bookshop or reference library.

Barry, Jonathan and Jones, Colin (Editors) *Medicine and Charity Before the Welfare State*, 1991.
Graham, Frank, *Northumbrian Castles: The Coast*, 1972 (reprinted 1978).
Goodall, John, (English Heritage), *Warkworth Castle and Hermitage*, 2006.
Linsley, Stafford, *Ports and Harbours of Northumberland*, 2005.
McAndrews, T. L., *Amble and District*, 1912 (reprinted 1996).
Morrison, Paul and Rylance, Tony, *Amble: The Friendliest Port*, 1988.
Rippon, Bartle, *The Amble Branch*, 2007.
Wilkinson, David and Kennedy, Glyn, *Amble: A Short History*, 1989.
Wilkinson, David and Morrison, Paul G., *A Story of Amble*, 1985.
Wilkinson, David and Morrison, Paul G., *Coquet Island*, 1989.

INTRODUCTION

By any measure of recorded history Amble is new and Warkworth is old. The most obvious pointer to Warkworth's age is the castle, a monument to the menace of border warfare, but those troubled times also affected other elements of the village notably the Church of St. Lawrence where the Earl of Fife is alleged to have massacred 300 villagers who had sought sanctuary there in 1174. He also burned the village. The bridge had a gatehouse to keep the Scots at bay, but its more regular daily function was to make it easier for people to travel, do business and get on with their lives. The way folk lived can be gauged from the narrow burgage plots behind the houses, but village fortunes were so closely tied to those of the castle and its occupants that when the great walls were finally deserted, there was little expansion beyond the old limits. The coming of the railway, and a station situated a mile away, also had little impact except in the summer season when large groups of campers swelled the population.

For over a hundred years Amble thrived, but the prospects did not look good when the industry it was mainly dependent on started to falter. By the end of the 1960s the pits had closed, coal shipments ceased and the railway was disused. At best, Amble's future was uncertain, but the town had one barely exploited asset: its position on the splendid north Northumberland coast and a proud reputation as 'The Friendliest Port'.

Increasingly, leisure craft have come to occupy the harbour while people who like to keep their feet on the ground are attracted by the seaside location. The little port that exploded into life in the nineteenth century is finding a new role for the twenty-first. Up river, the castle has become Warkworth's greatest asset, as invaders stream in from all directions intent, not on mayhem, but on adding to village prosperity.

If the railway effectively bypassed Warkworth, tracks were aimed directly at the mouth of the River Coquet. Prior to that, while Warkworth remained the principal settlement site, activities like fishing, farming and salt making were carried on, but in the 1830s, when coal mining began a few miles to the south it led to a transformation. The coal owners needed a place from which to ship the produce of their pits, but with no existing port, the river represented the best option for development. Within a decade, pits had been sunk, railway tracks laid and harbour works instigated. It was a massive and rapid change, and alongside the developing infrastructure a new village began to grow.

Initially Amble was small, but such was the scale of the mining and shipping industry that shaped it, that the village grew into a sizeable town and a separate ecclesiastical parish. Soon all the elements of an established community were in place: houses, churches, schools and shops. Some of these, notably the Co-op, grew to establish branches in the older towns and villages.

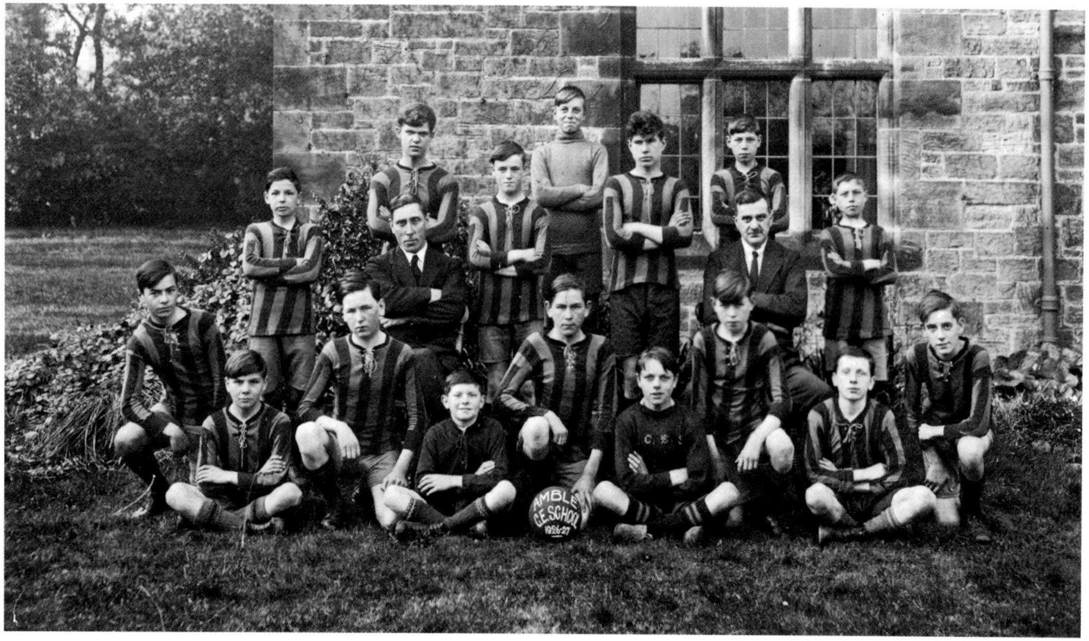

It's a leather ball, not a crystal one, but the message is clear: these boys played football for the Church of England School in season 1926/27.

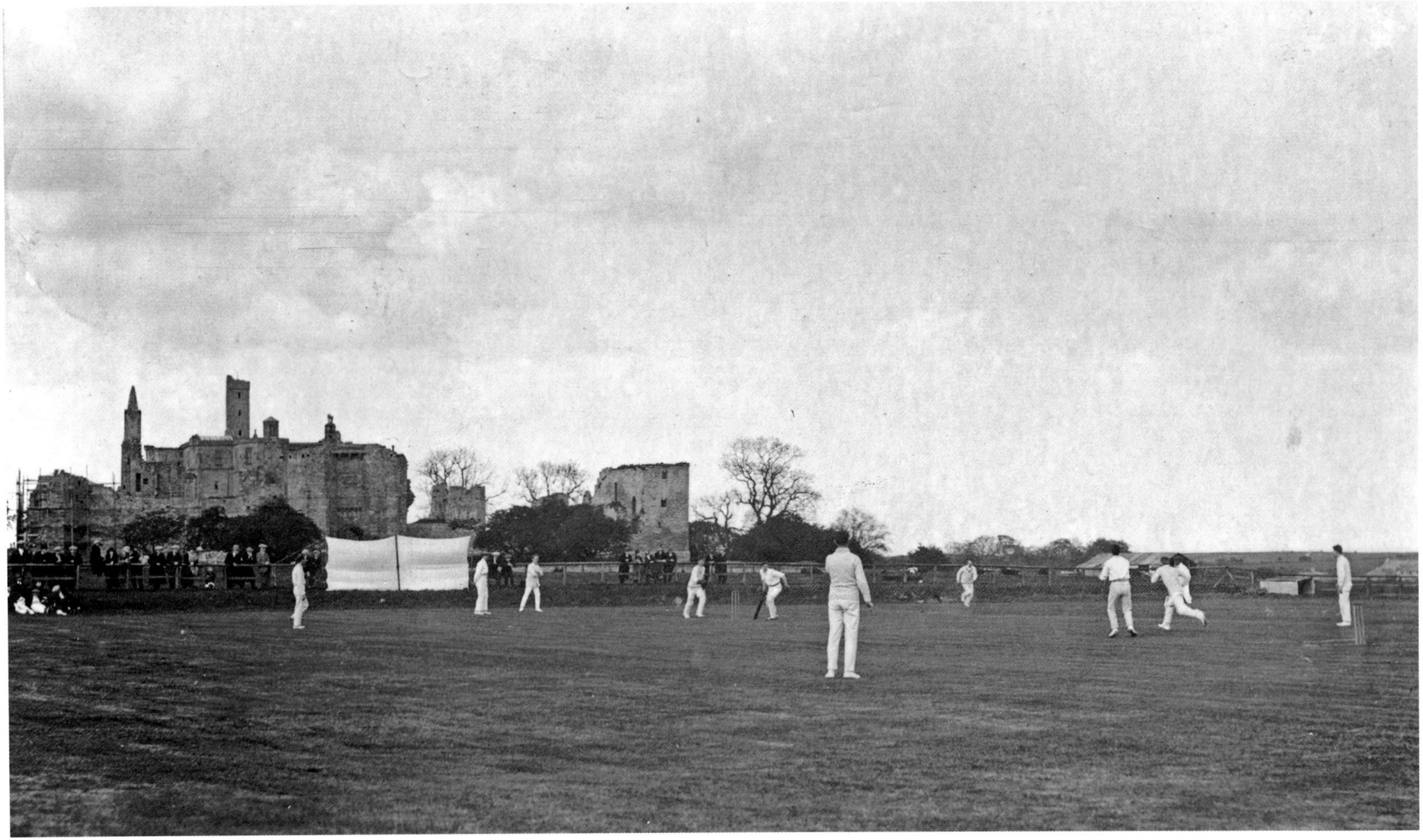

Built to withstand whatever ordnance a hostile foe could fling at it, Warkworth Castle, in this picture, appears to be at risk from nothing more dangerous than a well thwacked cricket ball. The game has been played in the lee of the castle since at least 1874 when Warkworth Cricket Club was formed, post-dating the castle by a few hundred years. Cradled by a horseshoe bend of the River Coquet, the castle hill was probably occupied in Saxon times, but it is not known when it was first fortified. Prince Henry, son of King David I of Scotland, who became Earl of Northumberland under the Treaty of Durham in 1139, has been credited with starting the process, but it is more likely to have begun after England's King Henry II re-possessed the earldom in 1157 and granted Warkworth to a Roger Fitz Eustace. With interests elsewhere, he left it to the mercy of invading Scots in 1173 and 1174, and so it was probably his son Robert and grandson John who began the process, early in the thirteenth century.

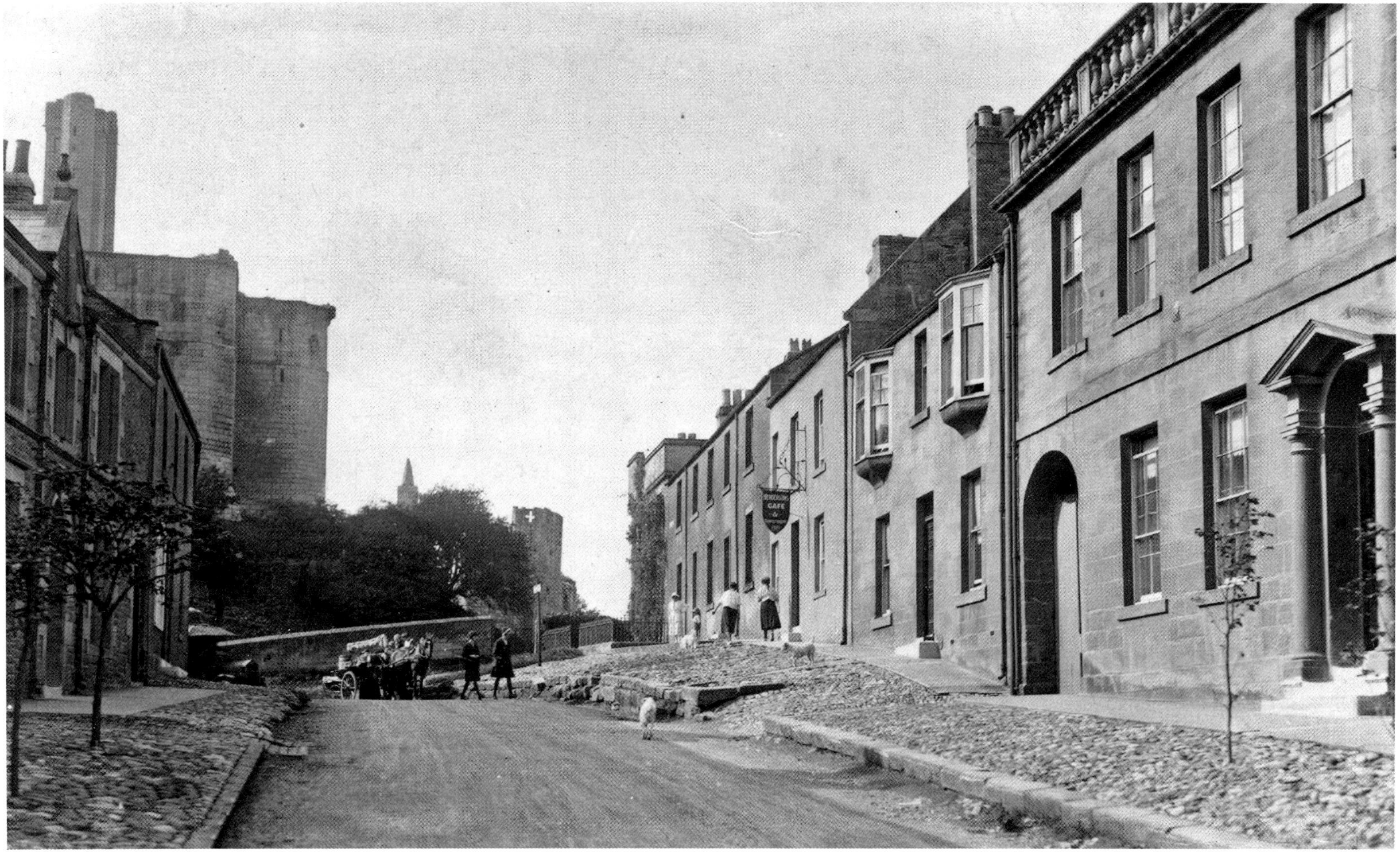

Warkworth and its owners found themselves in the front line of the wars triggered by King Edward I's attempts to annexe Scotland and amidst all the mayhem King Edward III granted the castle to Henry, the second Lord Percy in 1328. It was the start of a long association of the Percy family with Warkworth, punctuated by occasional interruptions owing to their tendency to get involved in rebellions, the most famous of which was perhaps when Harry Hotspur was killed at the Battle of Shrewsbury in 1403 when fighting against King Henry IV. Hotspur's father Henry Percy was made 1st Earl of Northumberland in 1377 and he is credited with building the most prominent element of the castle, the great tower, or keep. It is seen on the left of this picture, which dates from around 1900 and shows what the top end of Main Street would look like if modern motor vehicles disappeared.

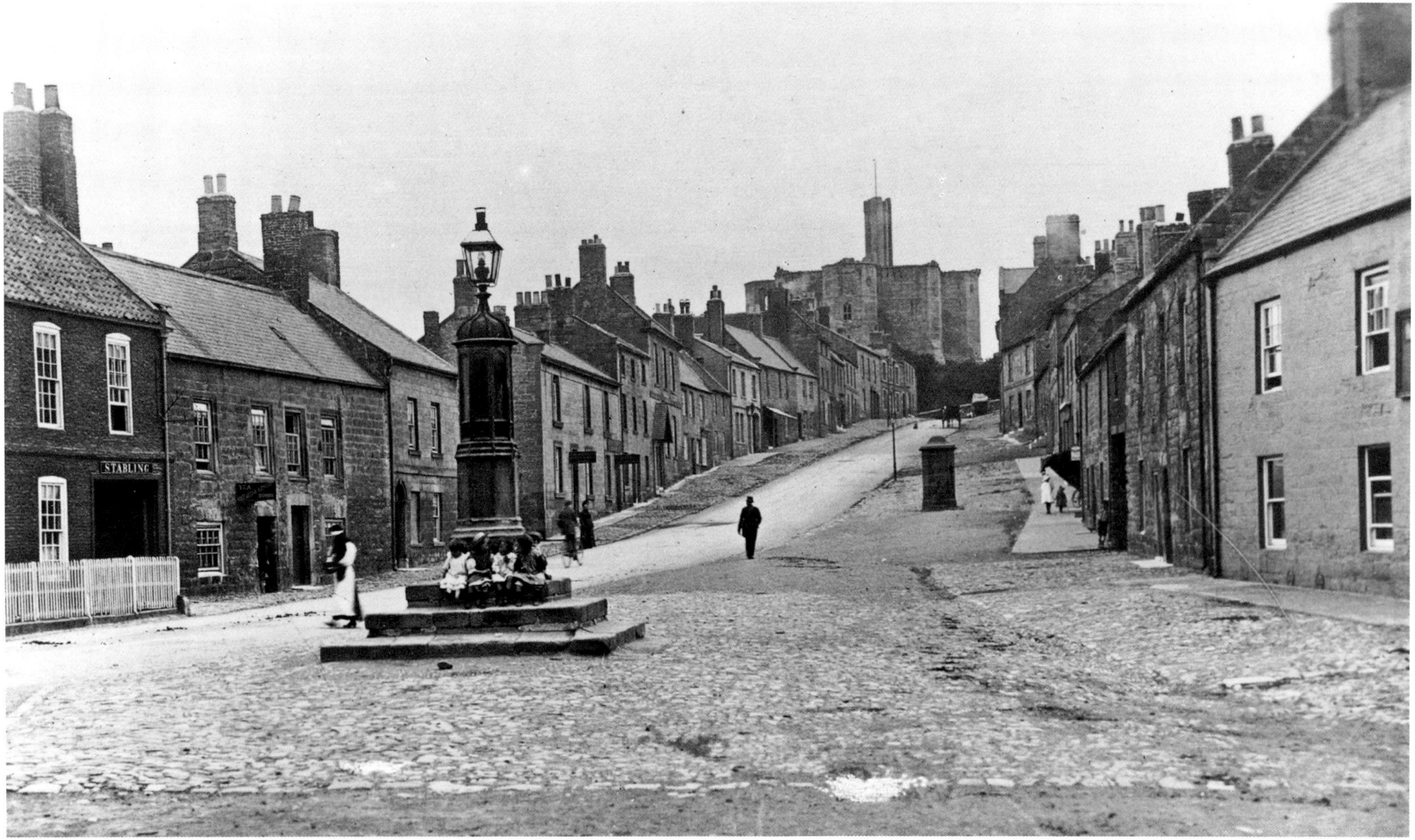

Protruding from the middle of the castle's great tower is a viewing tower that has been more visible since the upper works of the castle were shorn of chimneys, battlements, turrets and other decorative features. The progressive ruination of the castle began in the sixteenth century when it reverted to the crown following the death of the childless sixth earl and although the Percy family was restored after twenty years, the seventh earl was executed and the ninth earl imprisoned for associations with Catholic causes, and neglect of the castle continued. Parliamentary forces during the Civil War left it indefensible and in the eighteenth century cart loads of stone and other materials were taken away. The ruined building was partly restored in the nineteenth century, scheduled as an ancient monument in 1915 and taken into state guardianship in 1922. It is seen here at the top of the Main Street with the market cross at the foot of the hill in the foreground.

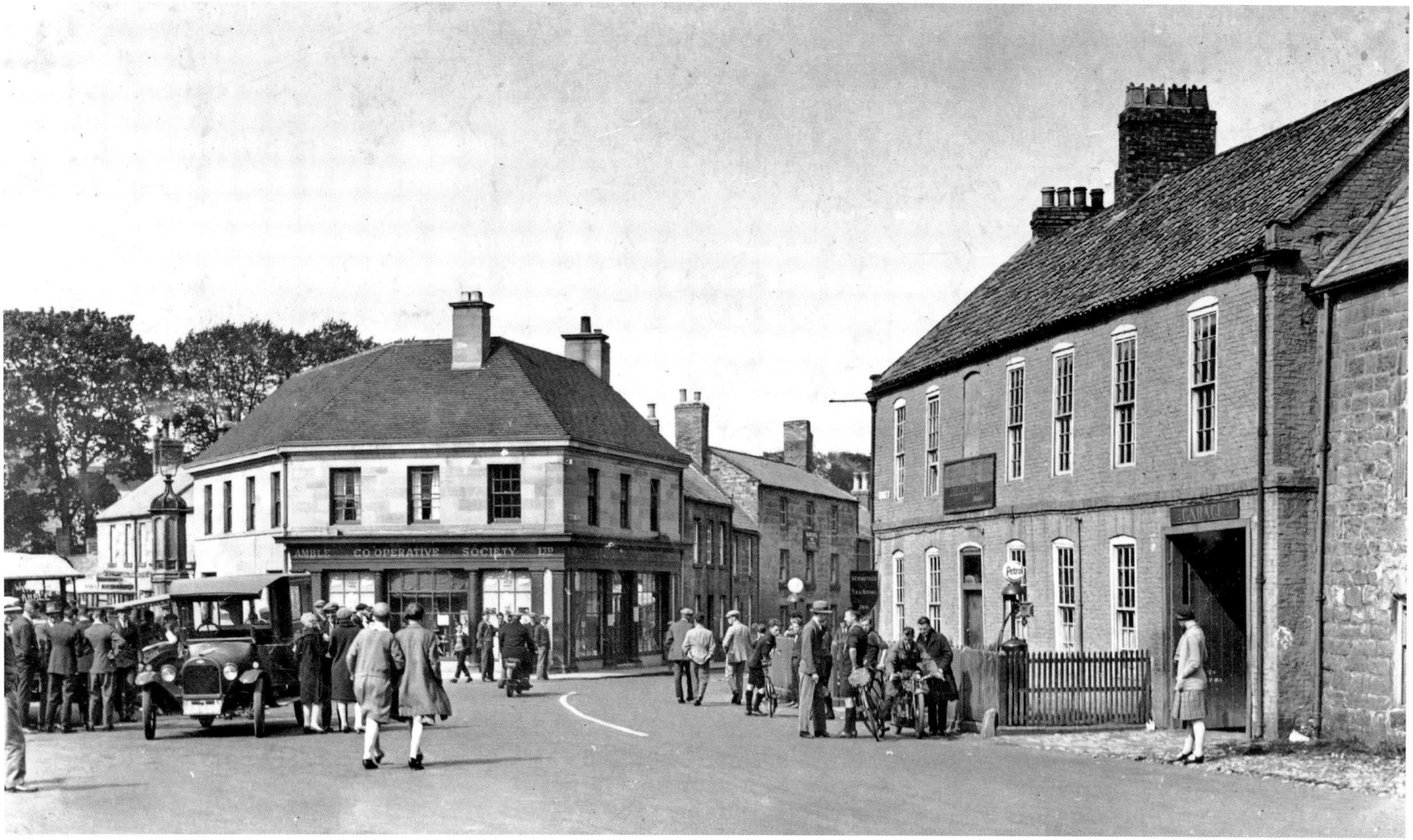

Warkworth has a typical medieval market town layout, with a castle at the top of a hill, a main street running down to the market cross and square, and beyond that, the church, (out of picture to the left of this view). The market cross shown in these pictures sits on a base that dates from the early eighteenth century while the upper part was added by the Duke of Northumberland about 1830 and incorporates Percy family heraldic symbols on little iron panels. The picture, which was used as a postcard in 1927, appears to show, on the extreme left, a market in progress on the square, although the most obvious evidence for retail activity is the branch store of the Amble Co-operative Society. Formed in the 1870s, the society had a significant presence in Amble itself, but also had branches in Alnwick, Warkworth and some of the outlying villages. Bridge Street is seen to the right of the Co-op heading towards the northern entrance to the village.

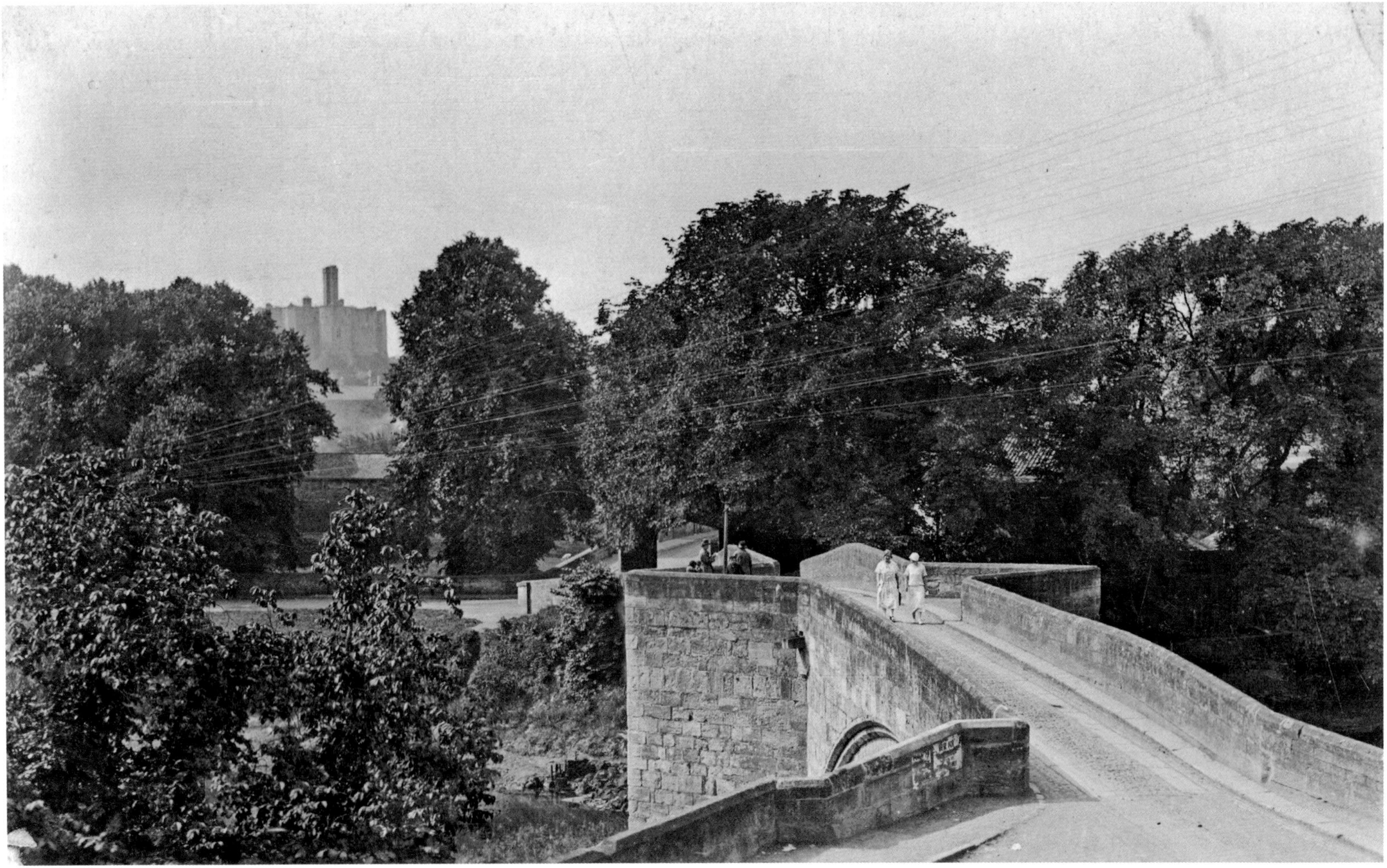

Erected in the late fourteenth century at much the same time as the castle keep, which can be seen through the trees on the left of this picture, Warkworth Bridge consisted of two stone arches supported by a substantial central pier. Large cutwaters on either side of the pier protected the structure from erosion when the river was in spate and also provided pedestrian refuges, which can be seen in the centre of the picture. As well as being a useful extension of the cutwaters, the refuges were necessary because, with the bridge 200 feet long and only eleven feet wide it could easily get congested with people, animals and carts unable to pass each other. Another measure designed to protect the bridge from erosion was paving on the river bed around the central pier.

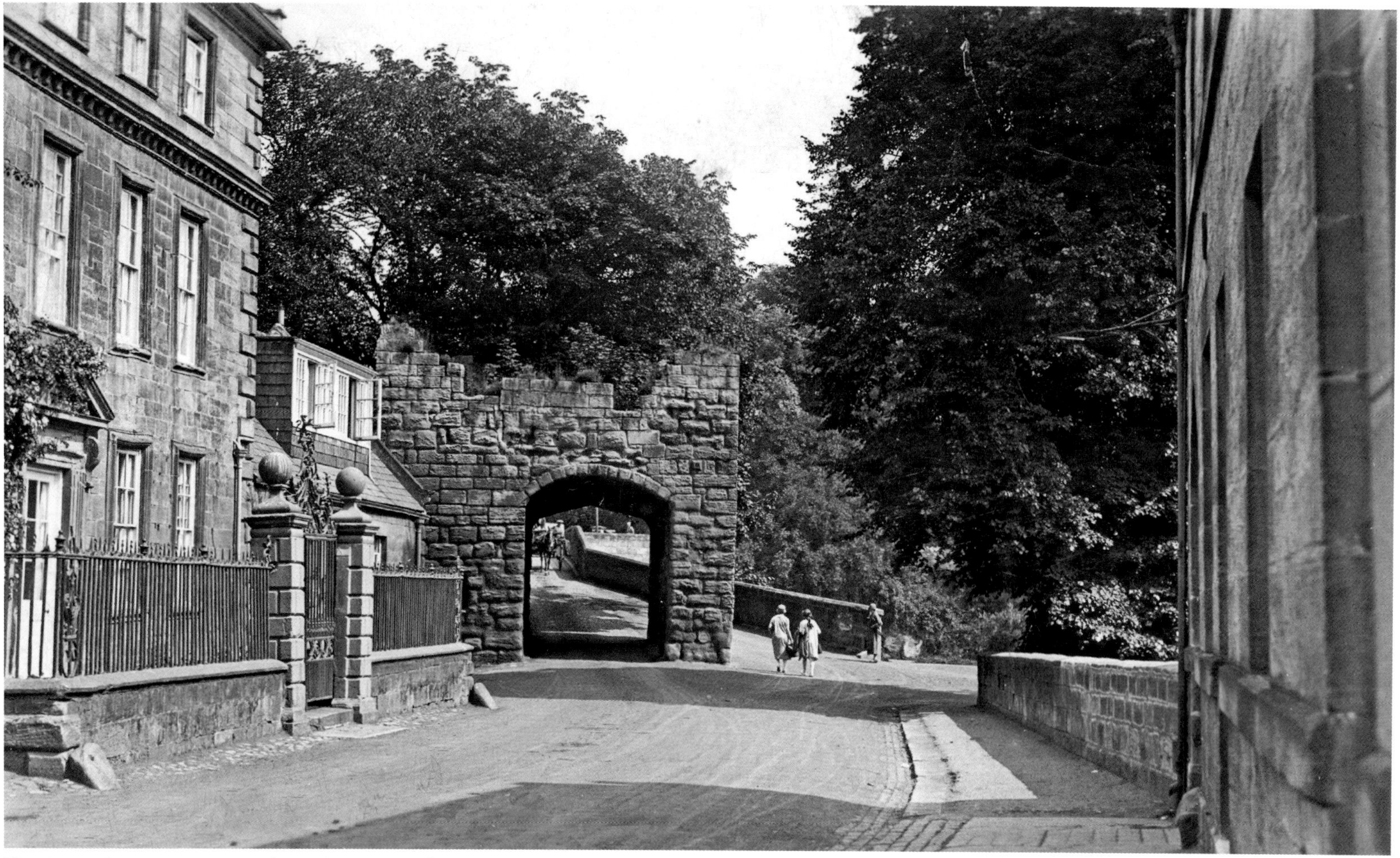

The River Coquet was a significant barrier, so the bridge was an important link in the road along the east coast, but it was also a potential weakness in the defences of both town and castle. To protect this 'back door', a guardhouse was built across the southern end of the bridge, so that it could be closed should a threat appear from the north – as threats in the form of marauding Scots tended to do when the bridge was built. The likelihood of this happening had long since receded when, as this picture shows, the gate tower was bypassed. This quaint old fashioned arrangement persisted well into the motor age and the medieval bridge was still in use by vehicles up to 1965 when a new bridge, built alongside the old, was opened. In a metaphor for the time, stone from the railway station at Longhoughton, which had been closed in 1962, was used to build the retaining wall for the embankment on the north side.

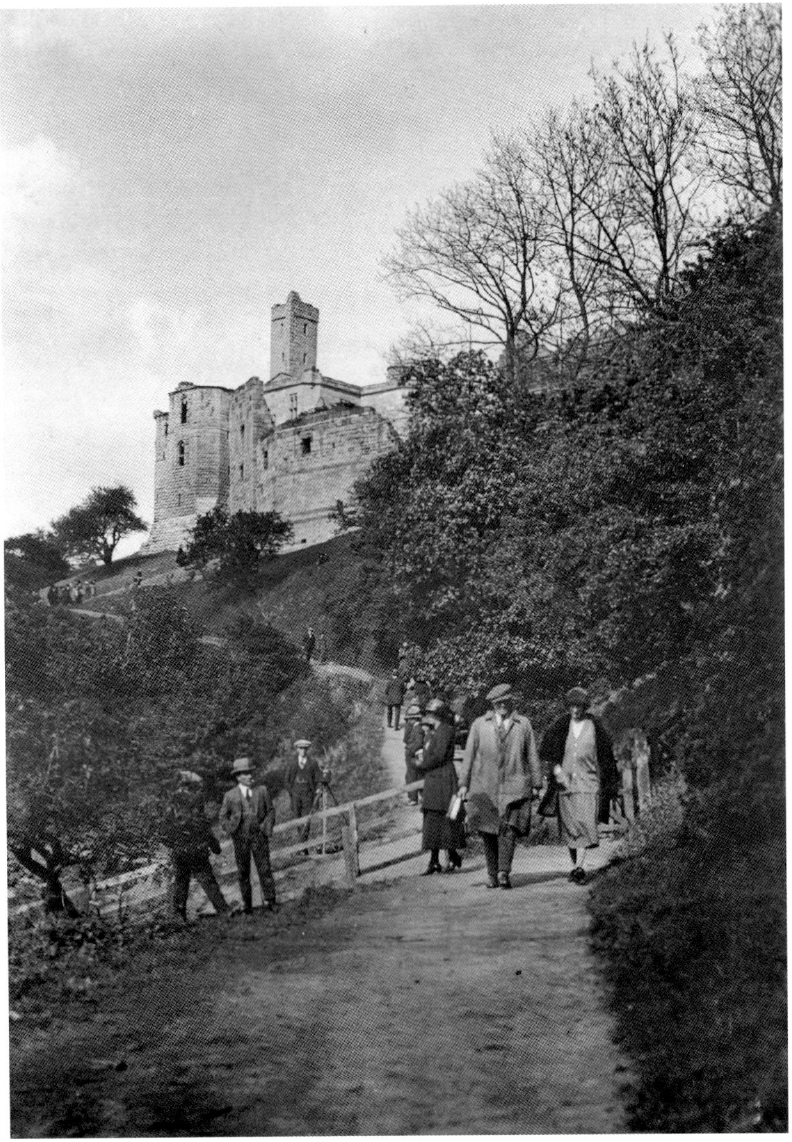

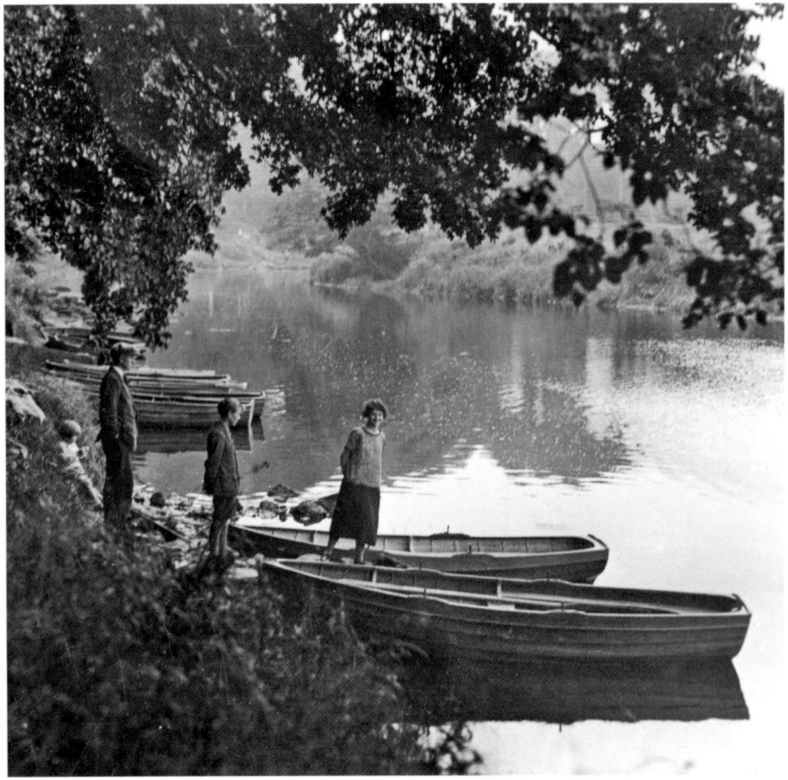

The Coquet wasn't just a first line of defence for Warkworth and its castle, it was a good salmon and trout river, so it also provided food and some income from the sale of fish. Tidal to a point about a mile above the bridge its level was fixed in a series of pounds by weirs, mostly associated with mills – Morwick Mill was a favourite spot for Sunday school picnics. Boating on the river was both a necessity, for fishing, and also for pleasure as tourism developed during and after the Victorian years, as these pictures of the boating station, and the path from the castle show. A boat was also a good way of getting to the Hermitage, a remarkable chapel cut out of the cliffs on the opposite bank of the river to the castle. Probably created at the start of the fifteenth century, it could have been used as a place of worship for about 150 years until such religious activity fell out of favour at the time of the Reformation.

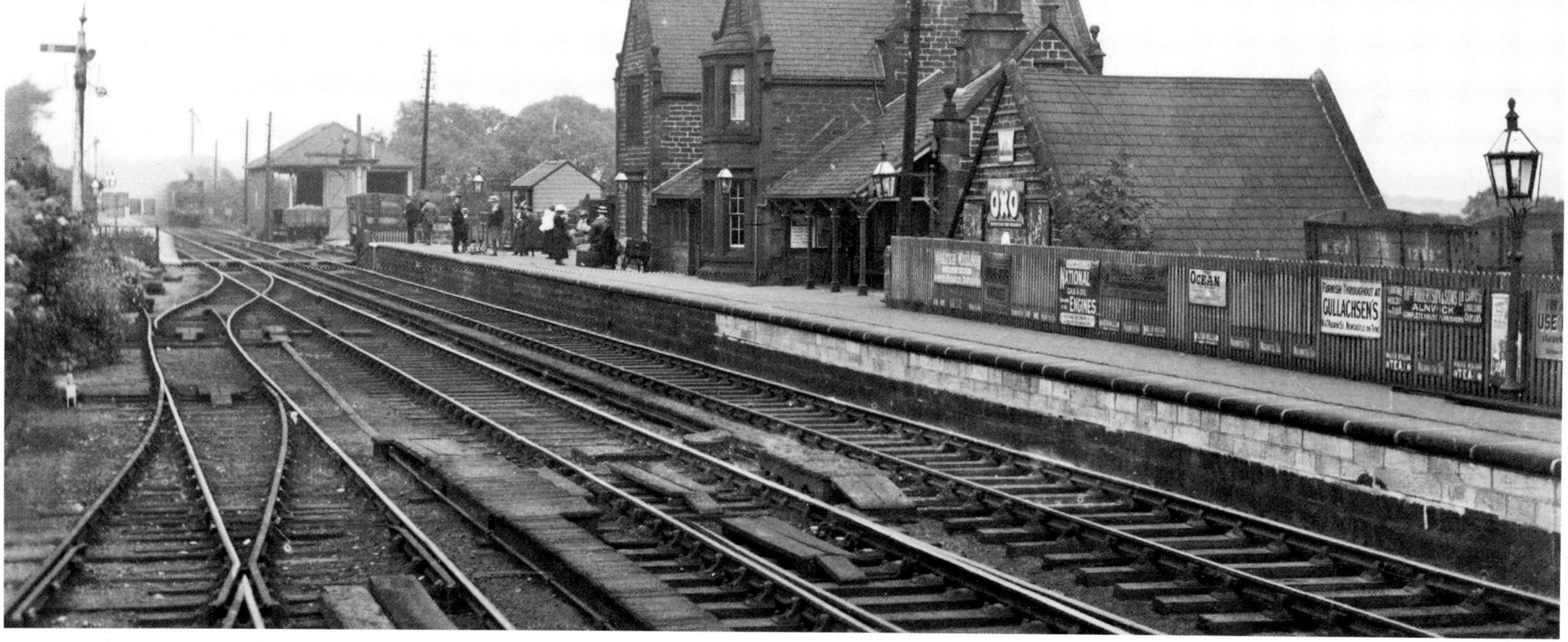

Warkworth Station, seen here looking north, was situated about a mile to the west of the village. A grand structure with an imposing entrance from the road, it was built to the designs of Benjamin Green for the Newcastle and Berwick Railway, which opened in 1847. The company was one of a number that constructed the east coast main line between London and Edinburgh, a link that was completed in 1850 with the opening of the Royal Border Bridge at Berwick. The Newcastle and Berwick became part of the North Eastern Railway in 1854 and when the railway companies were grouped under four large concerns in 1923, the line became the central core of the London & North Eastern Railway (LNER). Nationalisation followed in 1948, but for Warkworth, an isolated country station on a busy main line, there was only going to be one future. It was closed to passengers in 1958 and to goods traffic four years later.

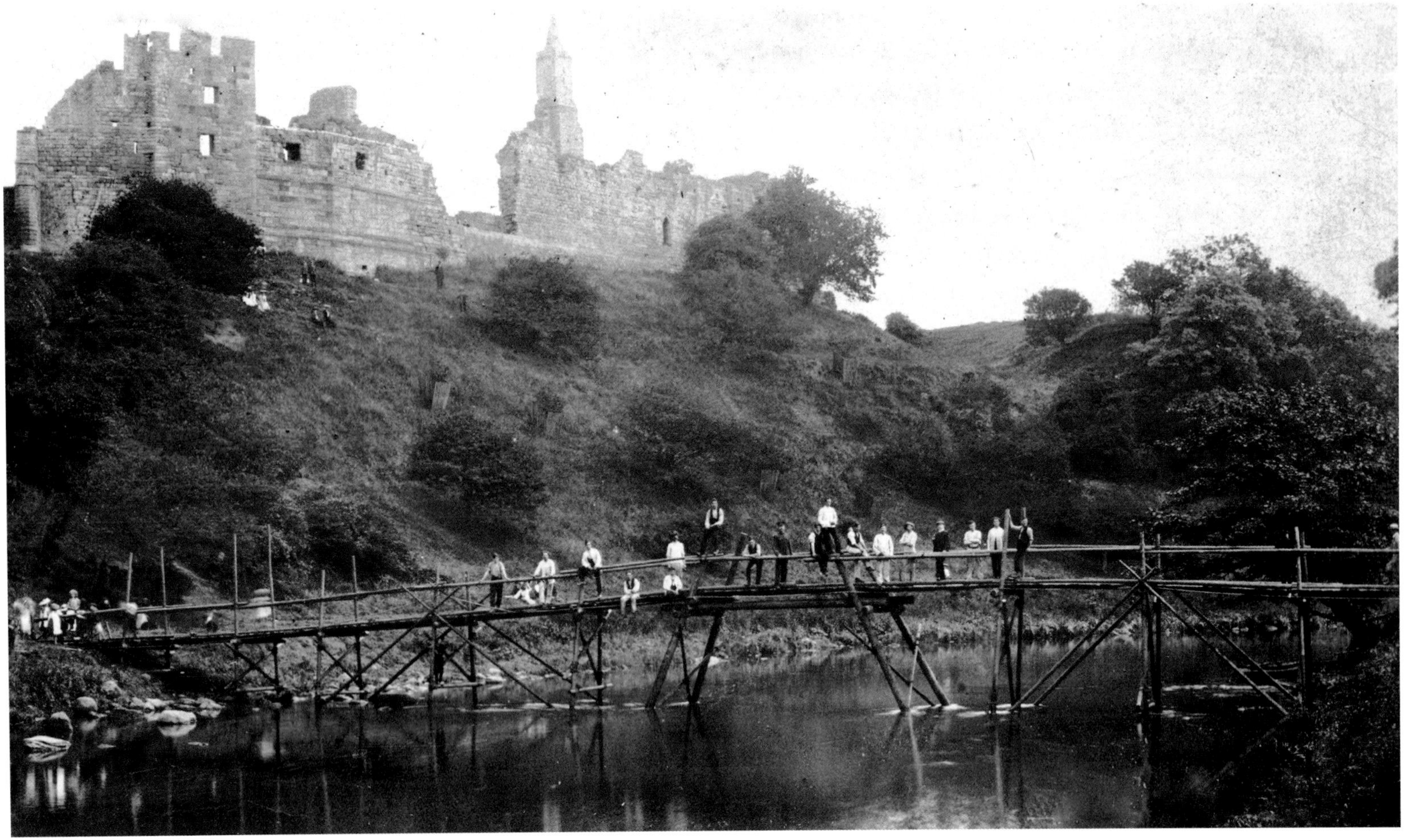

A number of youth organisations were formed in the late nineteenth and early twentieth centuries with the aim of giving young people a structured and meaningful outlet for their energies. One of these groups was the Church Lads Brigade, started in Fulham in 1891. Its influence spread rapidly and by August 1906, when the Brigade's North Eastern Camp was held at Warkworth, around 1,500 boys came to it from all over the northern counties. They arrived at Warkworth Station in special trains and, when assembled, proceeded in perfect order to the campsite across the river from the village, but linked to it by this temporary bridge. It was after midnight when they were allocated to their tents and bedded down for the first night. They had little time to dream because reveille was at 5.30am: there was quite a strong military flavour to the way the activities were conducted under the command of Colonel Hugh Brown of the 1st Volunteer Battalion of the Durham Light Infantry.

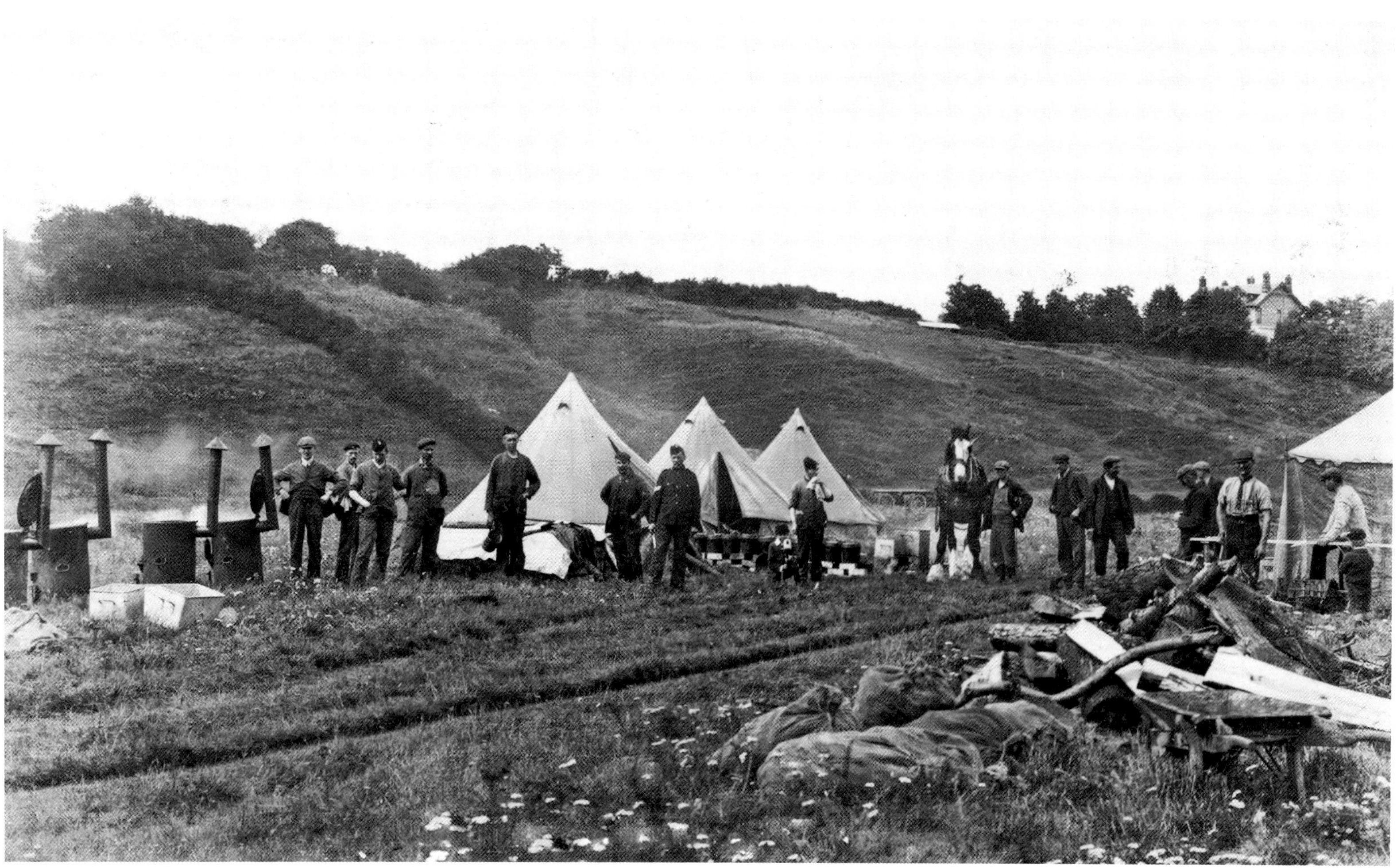

The military influence is evident in the clothes worn by some of the adult helpers seen here at the camp's field kitchen. Catering for so many boys was a big logistical task. Having been roused from their brief slumber, the lads were given coffee at 5.45am, breakfast at 8.00am, dinner (lunch) at 12.45pm and tea at 5.00pm. Daily consumption of produce was prodigious: 700 loaves of bread, 300 pounds of fruit cake, 800 pounds of beef, 12 hundredweight of potatoes, 2 hundredweight each of biscuits, cheese, sugar and bananas, 120 pounds of butter, 56 pounds of coffee and 28 pounds of tea. As well as the kitchens the camp had an 'institute', a large tent where the boys could relax, play games, read magazines and newspapers, and where sweets and lemonade were available. There was also a post office: messages home were sent through Acklington Post Office, which reported dealing with around 1,000 postcards a day.

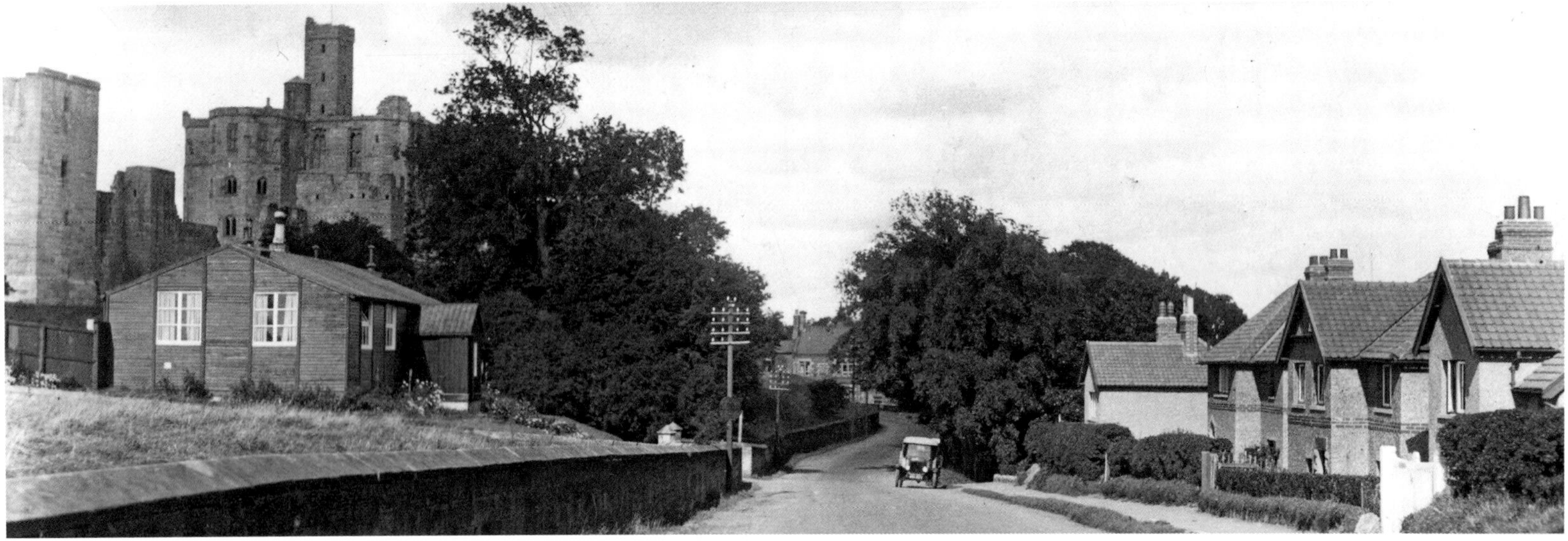

The photographers who took these views of the south end of the village trod much the same ground, with one picture showing the road outside the castle, while the other looks from the road across the river to Helsay. Both pictures were used as postcards, the upper one in 1930 and the lower one in the early 1940s, which almost certainly means it was taken in the 1930s. The houses where the Butts and Wellfield meet are on the left and although of a more modern period than the older part of Warkworth the land divisions are redolent of the burgage plots where, in medieval times, people grew food, kept chickens and possibly reared a pig or two. Trees have since grown up to obscure the view and modern housing has been built on the tennis courts and chicken runs.

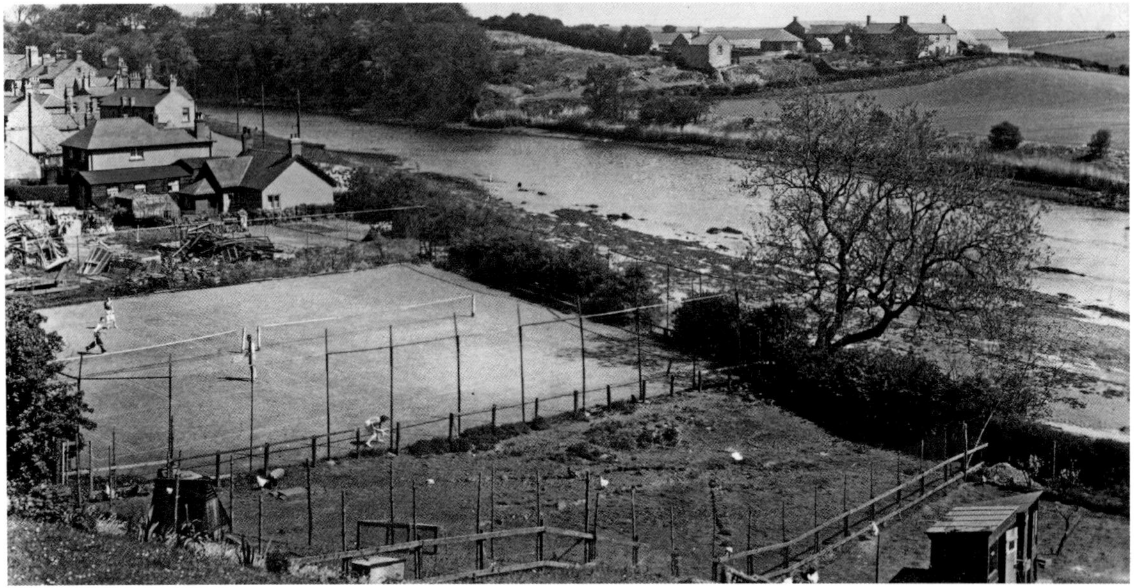

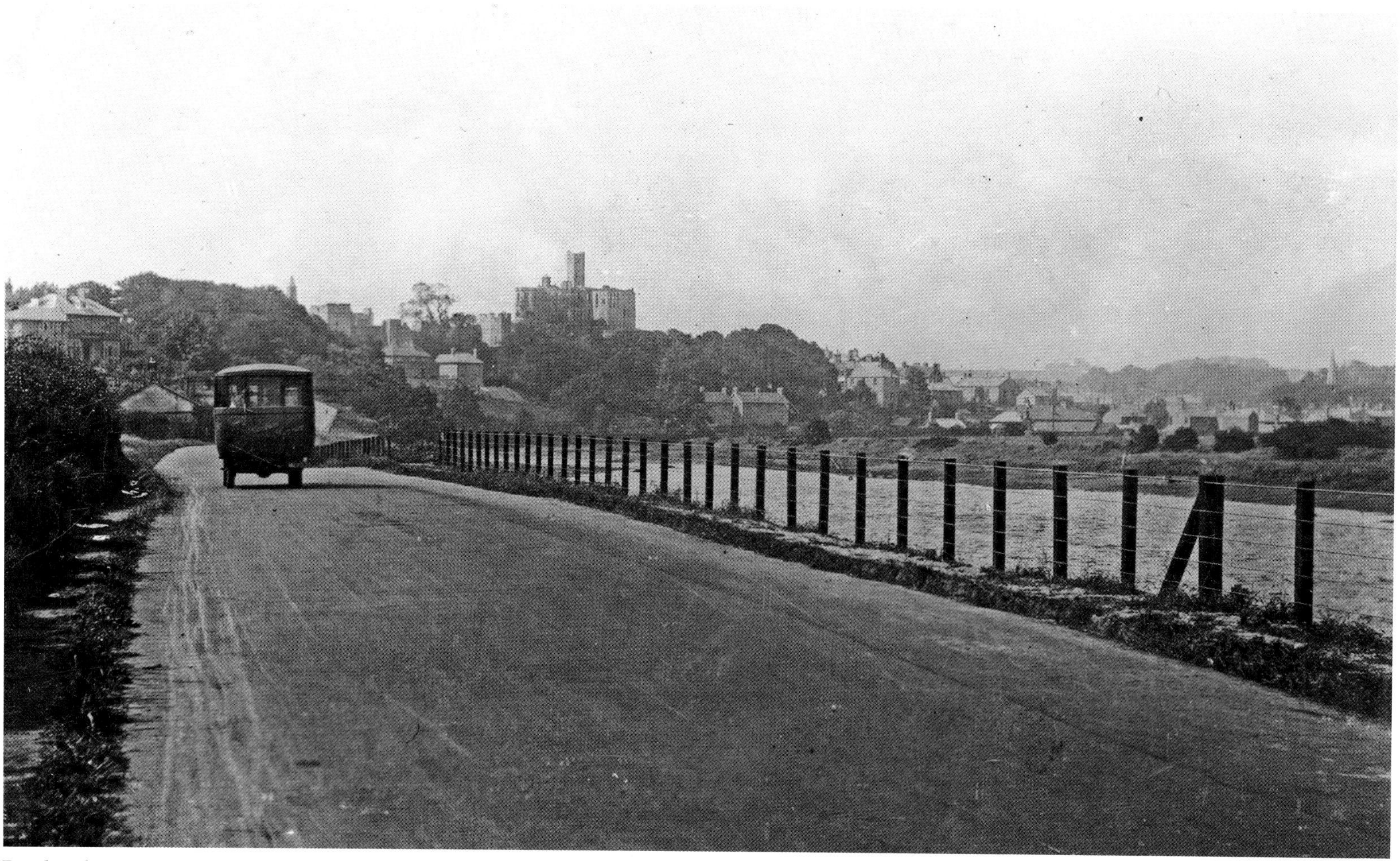

Road and river run side by side between Warkworth and Amble, as this picture from the 1920s shows. Since then, the road has been improved and raised to prevent flooding. The buses have also got bigger and although the river just keeps on rolling down to the sea, it hasn't always followed the same course. Before the development of Amble, the river's progress was slowed by the flat coastal plain and then impeded by a bank of dunes that forced it to swing up to the north for about a mile before finding a way out. All that changed in March 1765 when incessant rain and snow melt caused such a powerful flood that it broke through the dunes and created a new direct route to the sea. This new channel was then scoured out by the combination of river flow and tidal movements, a natural process that human beings would be able to build on to create the port of Amble.

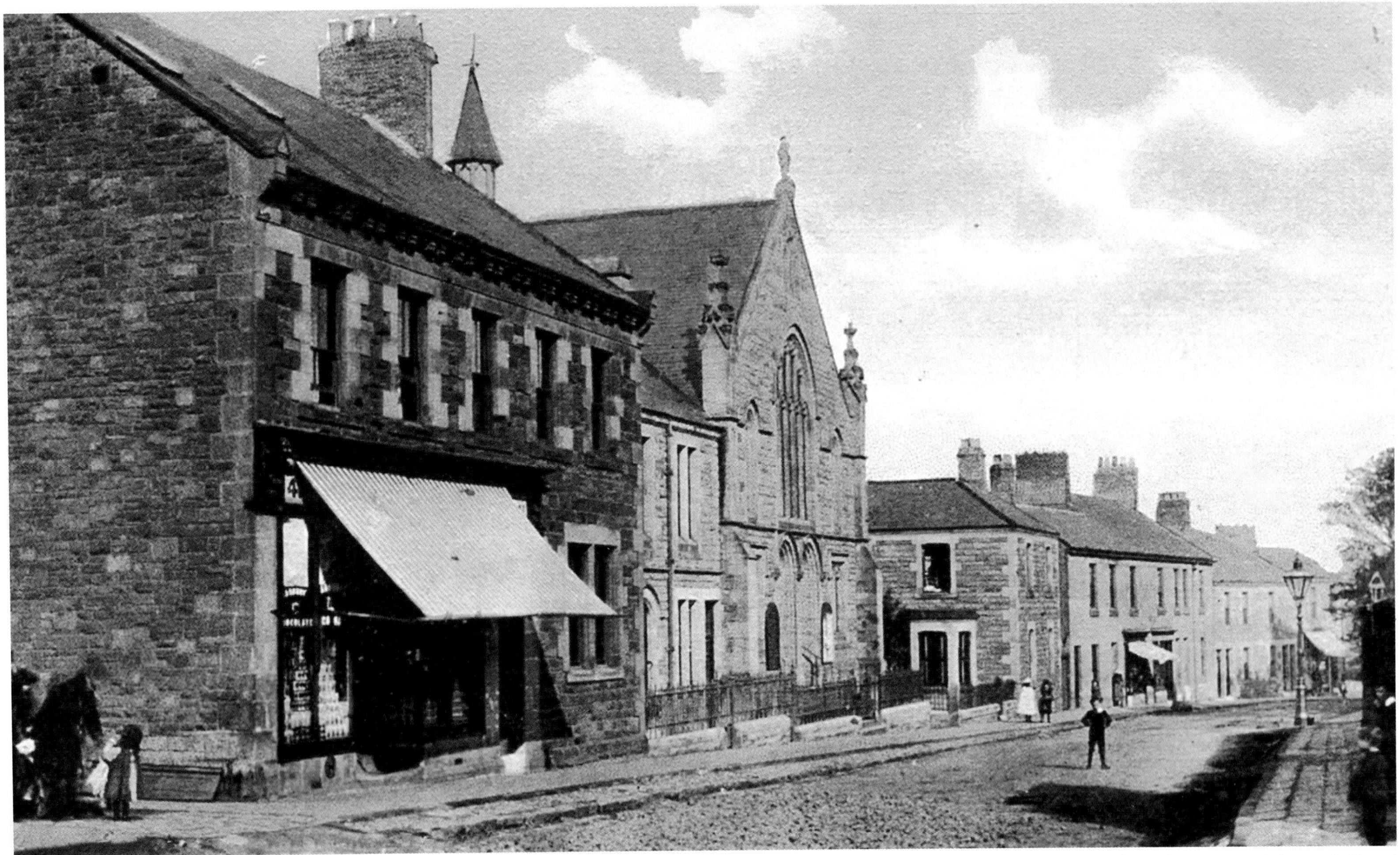

The Wesleyan Methodist Church was a prominent feature of High Street and was built in 1891, a hundred years after the death of the principal figure behind the Methodist movement, John Wesley. John, his brother Charles and George Whitfield were known as the 'Holy Club' at Oxford University where, as students, they developed a methodical Bible study form of worship. They remained within the Established Church, preaching around the country where their ideas formed the basis of local societies within parish churches. John Wesley set up a conference to ensure that his work carried on after his death, but it took decisions in 1795 that hastened separation from the Church of England. Other strands of Methodism developed, but Wesleyan Methodism was the largest, its strong ethical values, based on Bible study, appealing to working people in industrial communities like Amble.

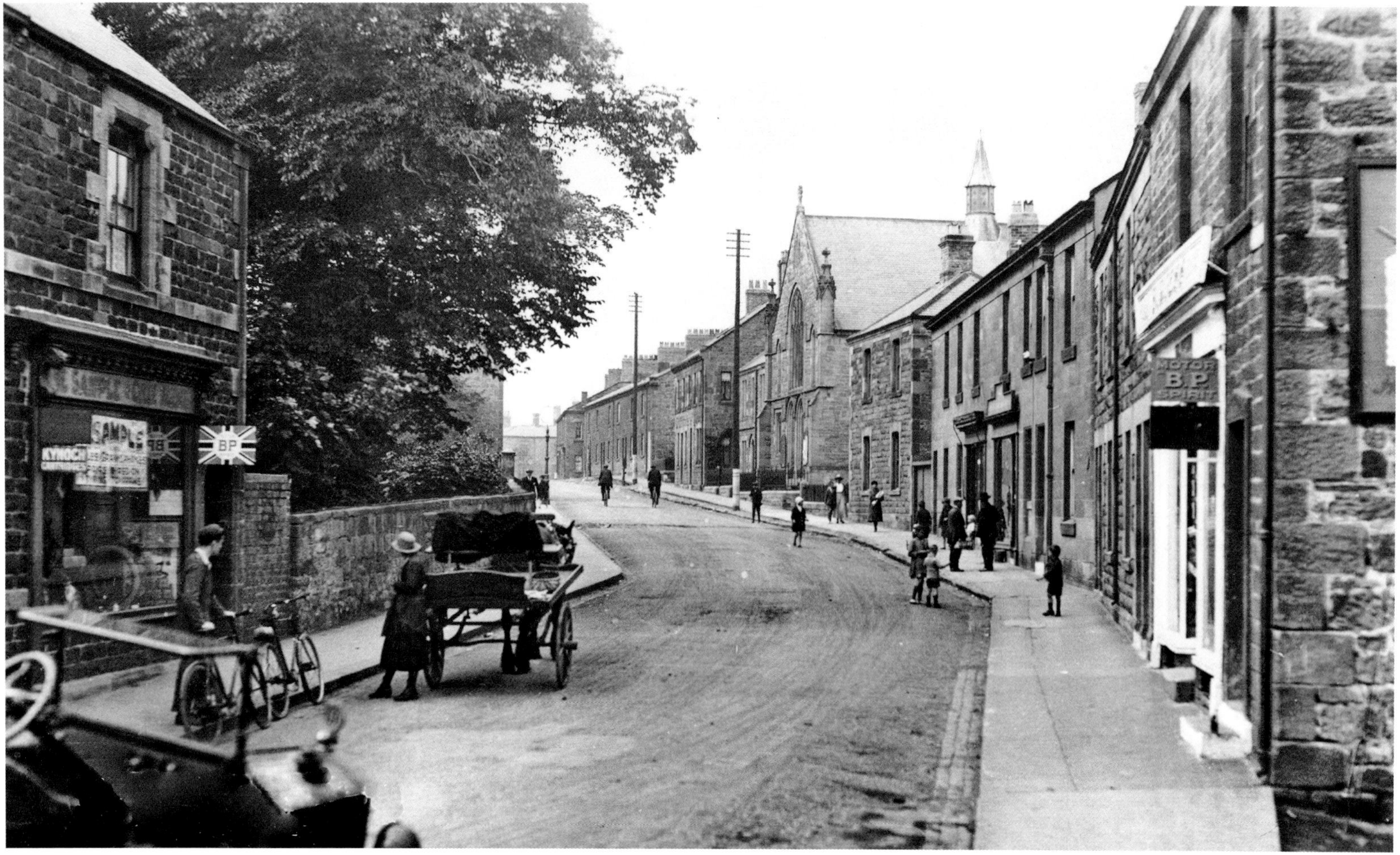

The Wesleyan Methodist Church is again prominent in this picture of High Street looking west, but it wasn't a view that would last because the church was demolished in 1972 after the structure was deemed unsafe. In the early years of Amble's development, High Street was the principal street, but with the rapid growth of the town it lost that status to Queen Street. Some shops continued to thrive and the two seen here at the lower end of the street have signs promoting BP products, but this is not what it might at first seem. The British Petroleum Company, to which the signs relate, was the marketing arm in Britain for a German company. It was taken over during the First World War by the partly state-owned Anglo-Persian Oil Company, which became the Anglo-Iranian Oil Company in 1935 and was renamed British Petroleum (BP) in 1954, some fifty years after this picture was taken.

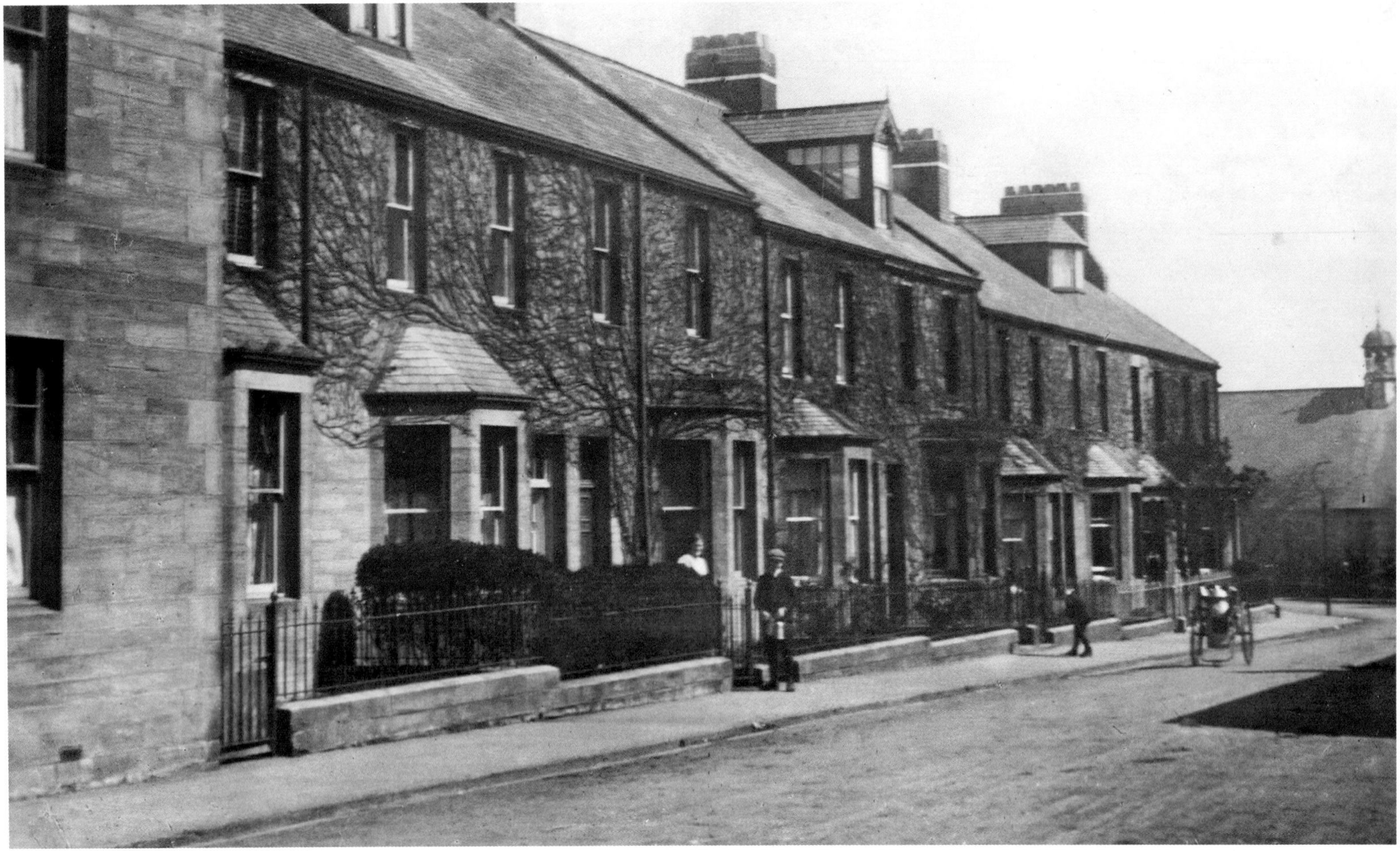

Bay windowed houses, with little front gardens, give Bede Street a more up-market appearance than neighbouring High Street. It is named after one of Northumbria's best-known historical figures The Venerable or Saint Bede, a monk regarded as one of the great scholars of the Anglo-Saxon period. Across the road from these houses is the Amble Club, also known as the Bede Street Club (what would the saintly monk have thought?). Founded as a social club in January 1902 it had, on the ground floor a bar, dining room and reading room, while upstairs there was a billiard room with two tables, a games room and bathrooms. Club members evidently enjoyed life, but took it seriously too as the tablets on the face of the building, commemorating those who fell in the twentieth century's two world wars, indicate. In the distance to the right of the houses is the Congregational Church.

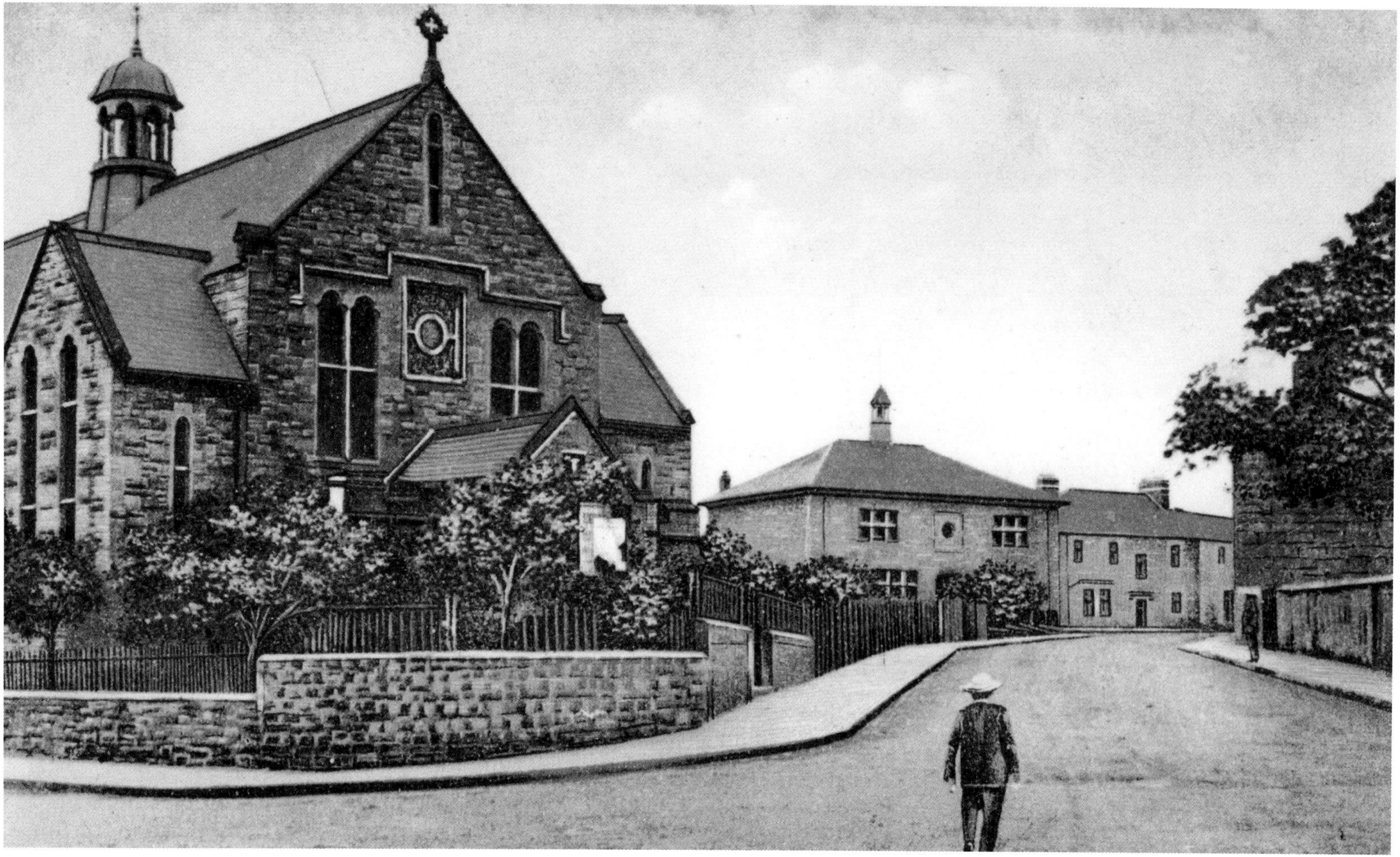

The Amble Club is in the centre of this view looking up Bede Street from its junction with Wellwood Street and will have been no more than five years old when the picture was taken early in the twentieth century. The Congregational Church, on the left, was built in 1894 to replace an earlier one, dating from 1845, in Gloster Terrace. Congregational Churches grew out of origins that go back to the Puritan, non-conformist religious movement of the late sixteenth century. Each congregation is independent and runs its own affairs, and churches see themselves as Christians who commit to God and each other, owing allegiance to no hierarchy. In 1972 the majority of Congregational Churches in England merged with the Presbyterian Church to form the United Reformed Church, and ten years later the church in Amble became known as St Mark's United Reformed Church.

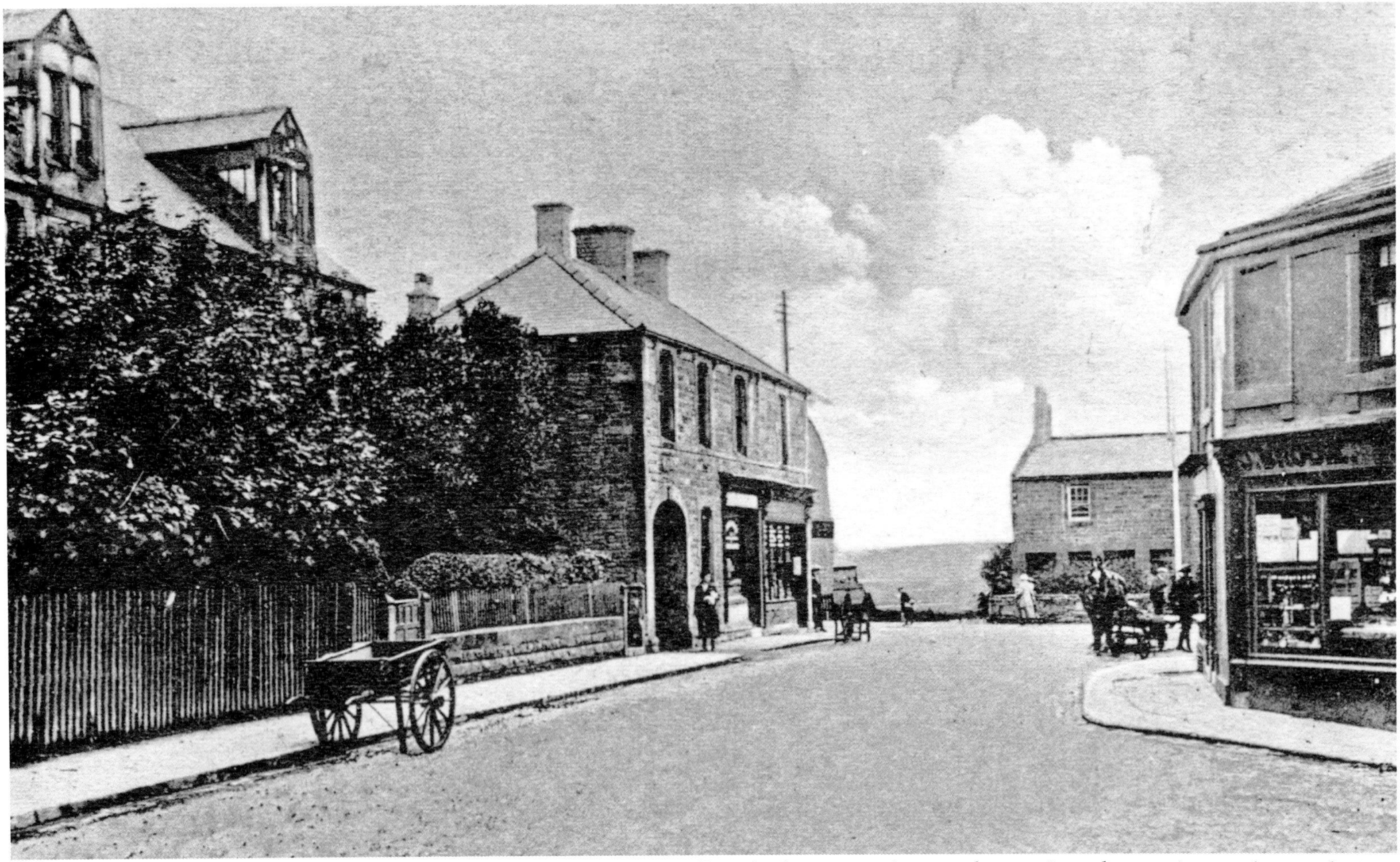

Much of Amble's housing was typical of nineteenth century industrial dwellings built in terraced streets that ran from the town's central core to butt up against the railway, as if it came as a surprise to the builders that they could go no further. Wellwood Street was one of these streets, but it was also, to use a sporting metaphor, a street of two halves and in this picture the photographer has chosen to ignore the housing and look the other way toward the Radcliffe Arms and the junction with High Street, Prospect Place and Queen Street. The junction with Church Street is in the right foreground. Wellwood Street, Bede Street, High Street and Albert Street also combined to encircle the eighteenth century Amble House, which remained in situ, overwhelmed by the growing town, until it was demolished in 1970.

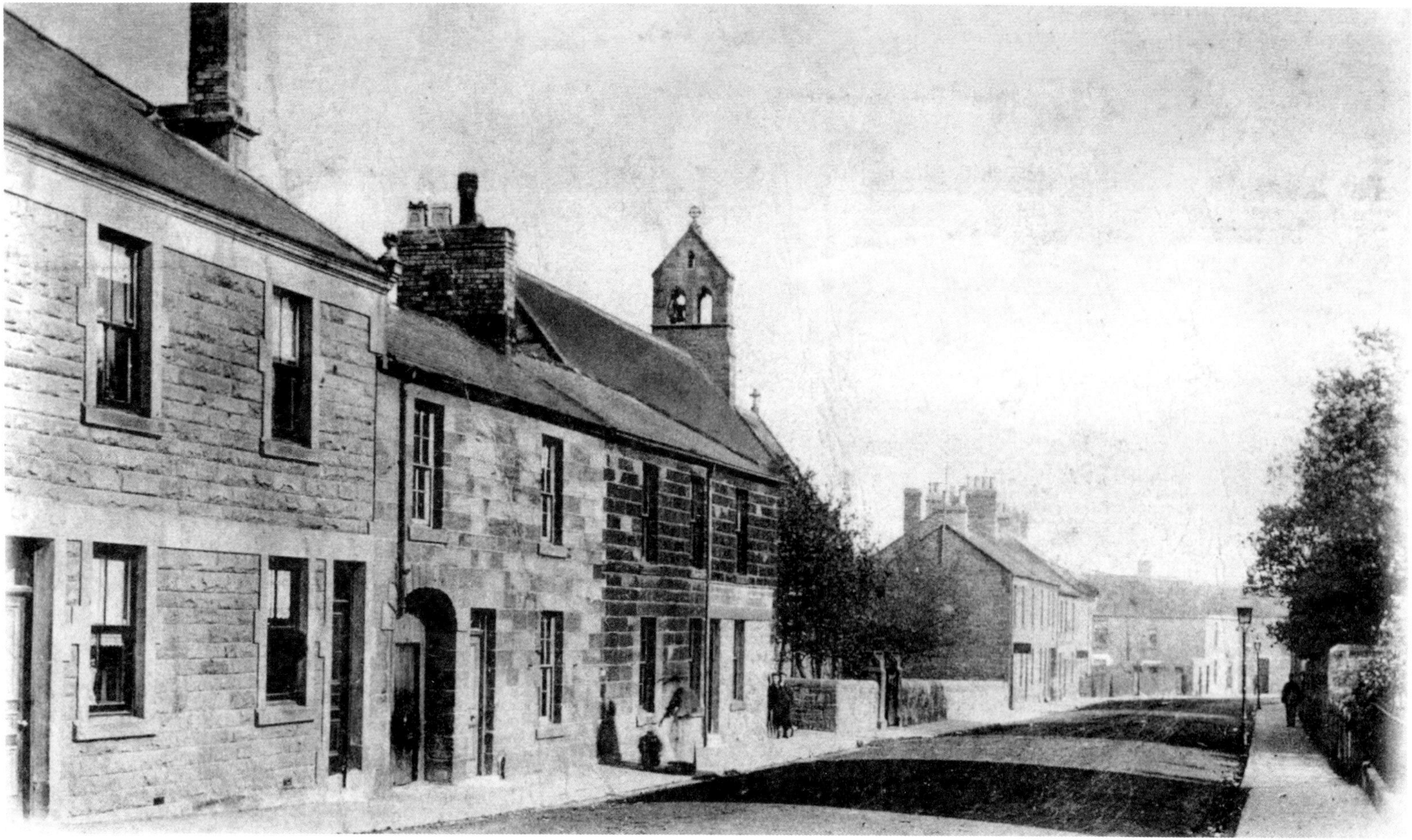

When development began, Amble was part of Warkworth Parish, but as the town grew that situation became untenable and in February 1869 a new ecclesiastical Amble Parish was created. The need for a parish church was quickly answered with the foundation stone being laid at the end of August. Designed by Newcastle architects Austin and Johnston and built by local contractor Robert Carse, the new St Cuthbert's Parish Church was consecrated on 18th October – St. Luke's Day – 1870. It is seen tucked in on the left of this picture of Church Street, with the location of the vicarage, on the other side of the road, indicated by the trees on the right. Perhaps the most poignant of the internal church fittings are choir stalls purchased by worshipers from the adjacent village of Radcliffe, and dedicated to their Chapel of the Good Shepherd, which was wrecked when a German aircraft dropped a landmine on it during the Second World War, just after the conclusion of a service.

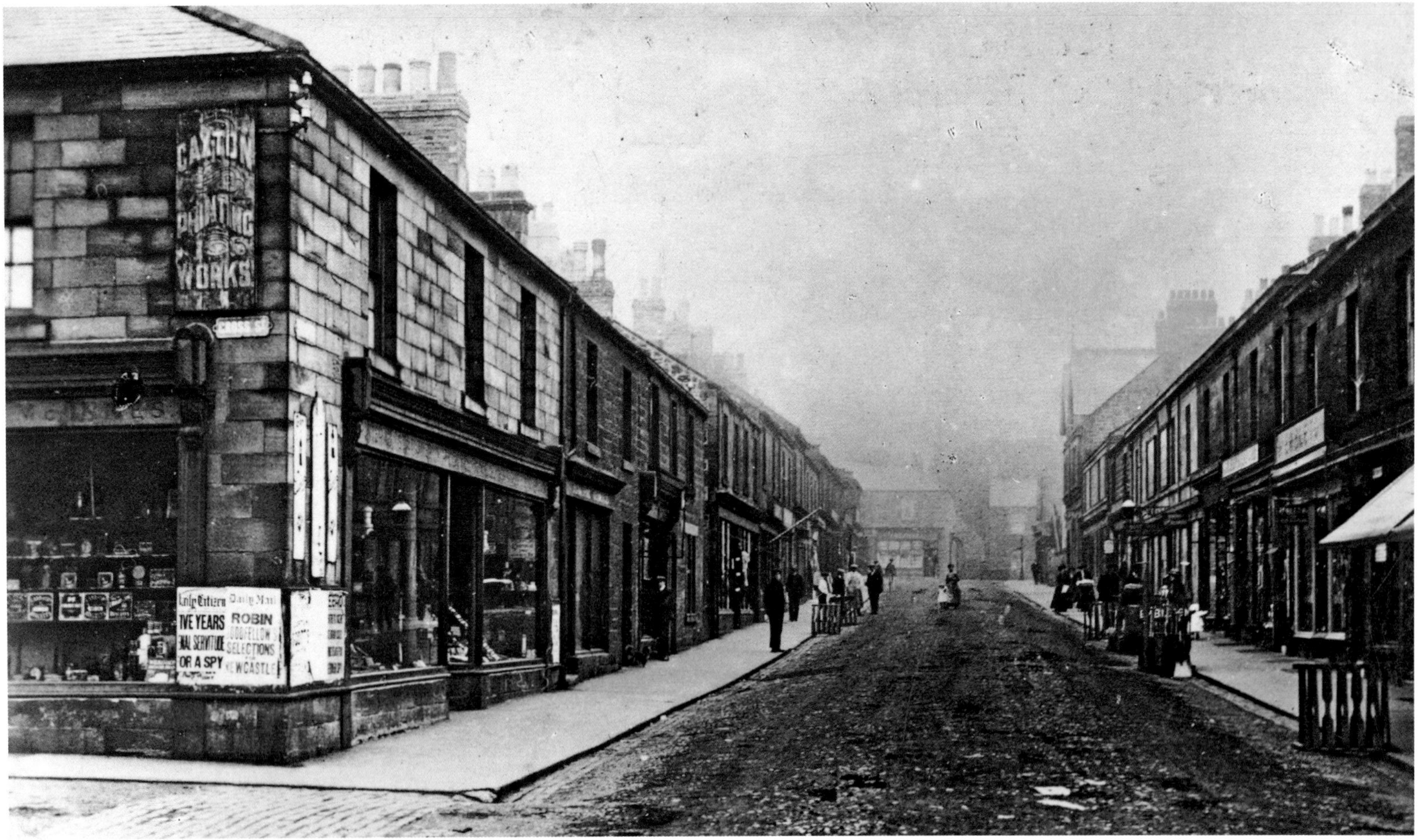

Amble doesn't pretend to be anything other than it is, a mid nineteenth century town with buildings that are firmly rooted in the vernacular style of the area making few concessions to flights of architectural fancy. This honest simplicity is evident in this view of Queen Street, looking toward Wellwood Street from Cross Street with Robert Green McInnes' stationery and newsagent's shop in the left foreground. The one exception to simplicity is the bank building, at the top of the street on the right, bigger and grander, and with its twin dormer windows standing tall. Across the street from the bank was Walter Willson's self-styled 'colossal business', a grocery shop that in its day provided stiff competition for the Co-operative store at the other end of the street. Changing times have seen the demise of Willson's grocery, the Co-op relocating to the top of the street and a large multi-national grocer operating where the old Co-op used to be.

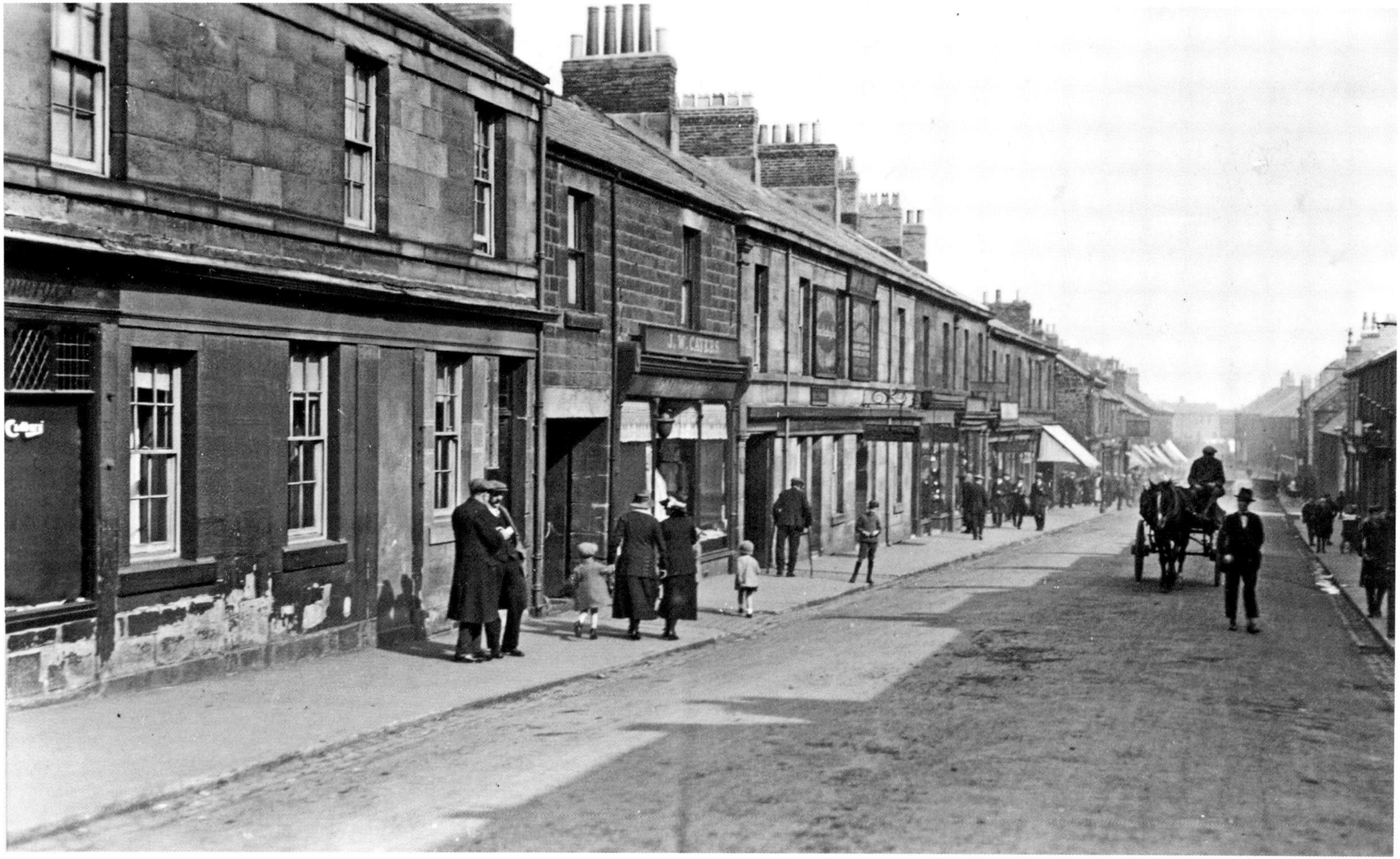

By way of a contrast to the picture on the facing page, this view shows Queen Street looking east. What the two images have in common is that they present a marked contrast to modern road and traffic conditions. The street surface is very rough and the combined total of vehicles is the single horse in this picture, dragging its cart up the hill in the opposite direction to the later one-way system and at a speed that is causing no concern to the pedestrian in front. In roughly the centre of the picture is the Dock Hotel, which like the Waterloo, on the other side of the street, has fronted Queen Street for decades. To its left, where the woman and children are walking, is Jane W. Cavers' drapery shop, one of a number of shops in the street run by women including milliners, Fannie and Nellie Walker, confectioner Jane Shaw and fancy draper Jane Gowland.

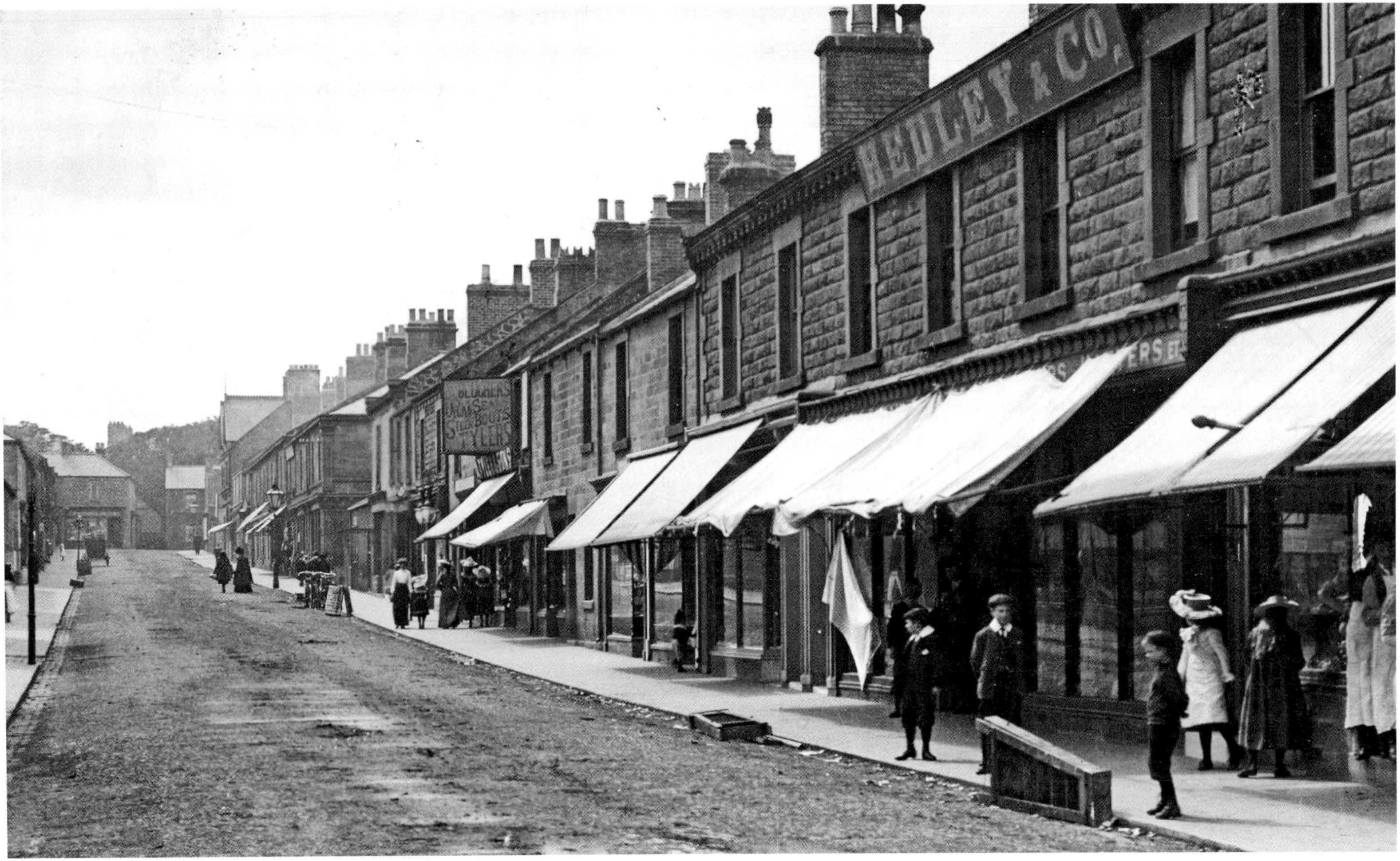

Looking west up Queen Street, this picture, used as a postcard in 1912, also favours the north side of the street, which because it faces south is basking, perhaps baking in the full glare of the sun. To protect their merchandise, shopkeepers have erected an array of blinds and awnings, but these have also hidden their identity from the camera. Two shops have prominent signs, Tyler's boot and shoe shop halfway up the street, and drapers and clothiers, Hedley & Co. Their awnings look dishevelled, as if they are being repaired or replaced and perhaps the two sets of stepladders lying in the gutter have been placed there while the photograph was being taken. There has always been a wide range of shops in Queen Street and long after these pictures were taken it continues to host a range of small independent shops, bucking the modern trend for shrinking diversity.

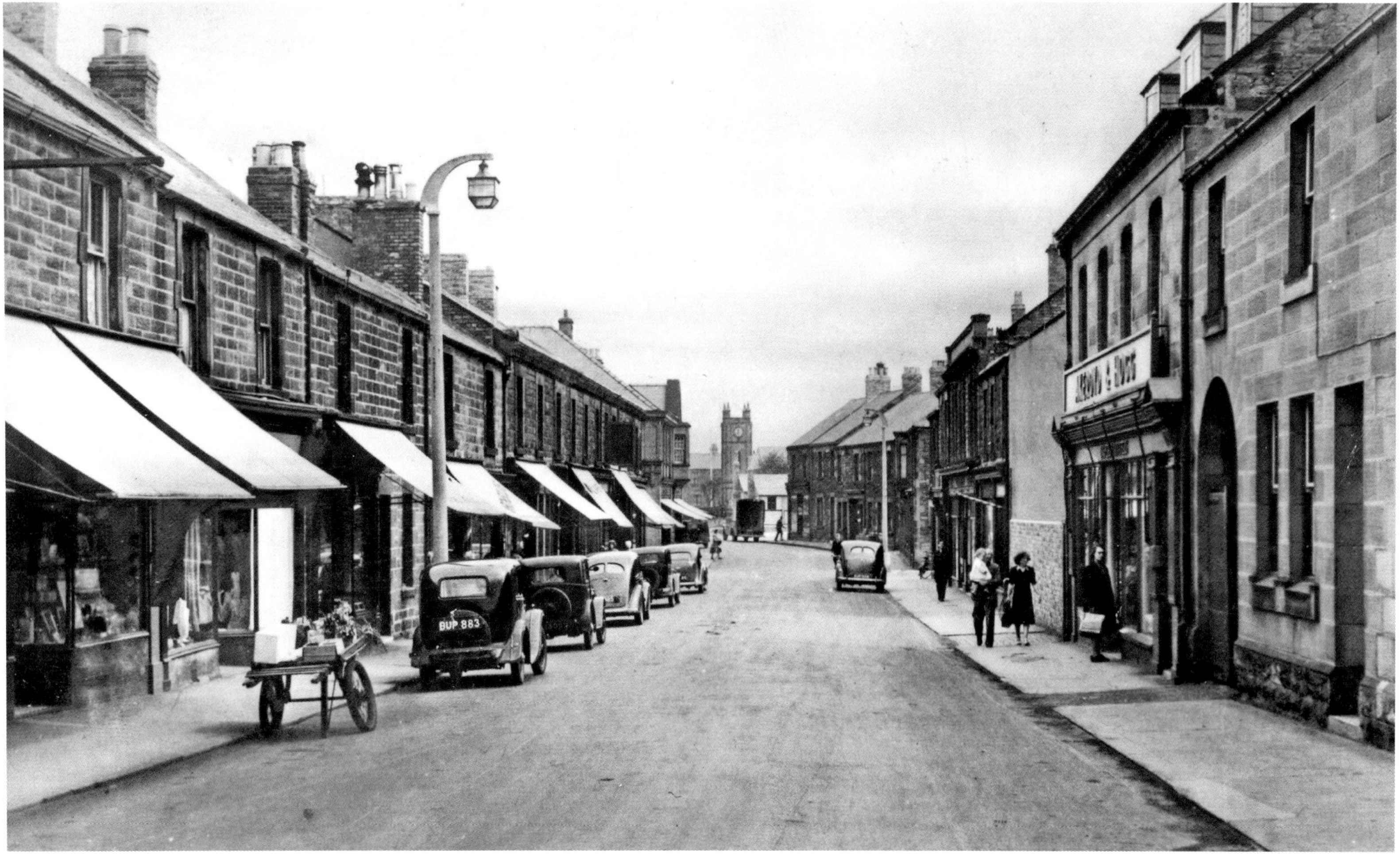

An increase in the number of cars is evident in this picture of Queen Street's eastern end taken around the late 1940s or early 1950s. The car on the end of the line on the left has an old style registration plate from County Durham. The shops on the left are, as on the previous page, protecting their windows from the sun with awnings – it's not that it was always sunnier in the past, it's just that photographers knew that they got better pictures when the sun shone. On the shady side of the street is the drapery and outfitter's shop of Akeroyd and Hogg, while at the foot of the street was another long-standing business, the Amble Co-operative Society. As well as its impressive headquarters in Queen Street, the society had branches in Albert Street, Bede Street, Leazes Street and Newburgh Street. In the distance, acting as a focal point, is the town's war memorial.

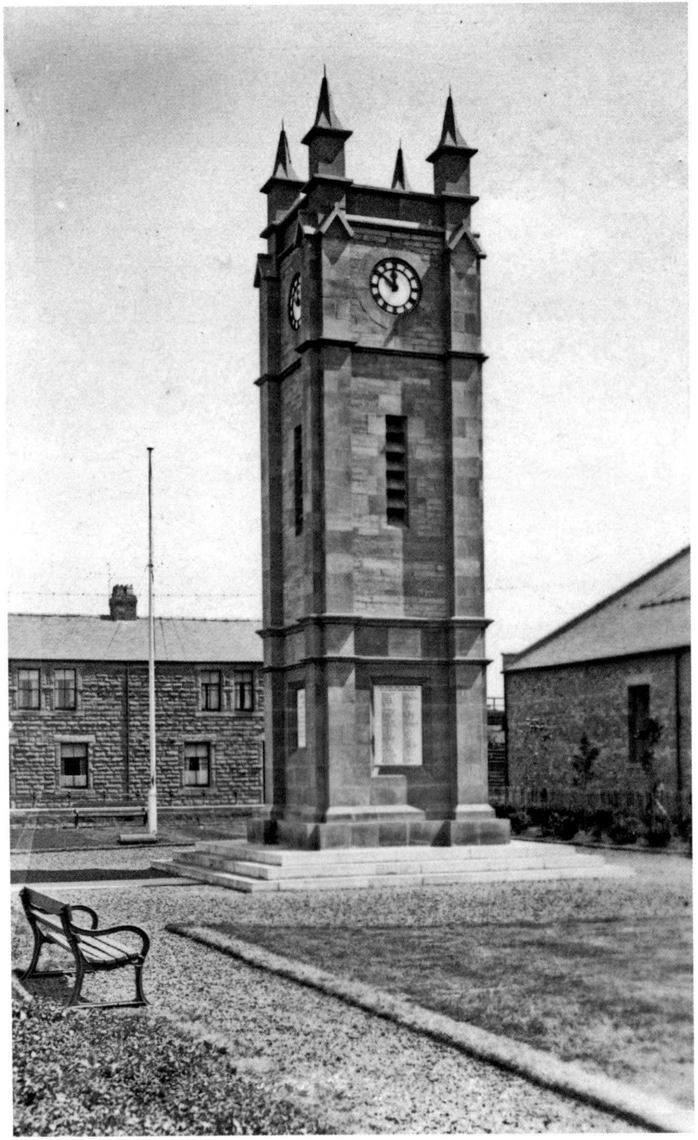

Amble's war memorial took the form of a 41 foot high, ten-foot square clock tower. It was designed by town surveyor W. Burton and erected by local contractor, R. Carse and Son using stone from Kenton Quarries, Heworth stone steps and Sicilian marble tablets, the clock was made by W. Potts of Leeds. The unveiling ceremony was held on 9th May 1925, attended by a crowd of over 4,000 people. It began with a procession through the town headed by the regimental band of the Northumberland Fusiliers, followed by C Company, Northumberland Fusiliers and the Amble and Radcliffe Band. Major Vernon Merrivale M.C. of Radcliffe, whose two brothers were named on the marble tablets, performed the unveiling and the Vicar of Amble, the Rev. T. N. Dunscombe, dedicated the memorial. A number of wreaths were laid, including one by Mrs. Tulley on behalf of the people of Amble. The ceremony concluded with a collection: a silver line laid along the boundary wall with the first coins being placed there by two children, Bella Turnbull and John Mackay, whose fathers had been killed in the war.

When Radcliffe was demolished in 1971 to make way for opencast coal operations, the central element of the village war memorial was removed and re-erected beside the Amble clock tower. Set on a raised platform with flanking pillars, the memorial is seen here in May 1928 after its unveiling by Lt. Colonel H. Liddell D.S.O., M.C. Amongst the wreaths was one laid by Mrs. Noble on behalf of the villagers.

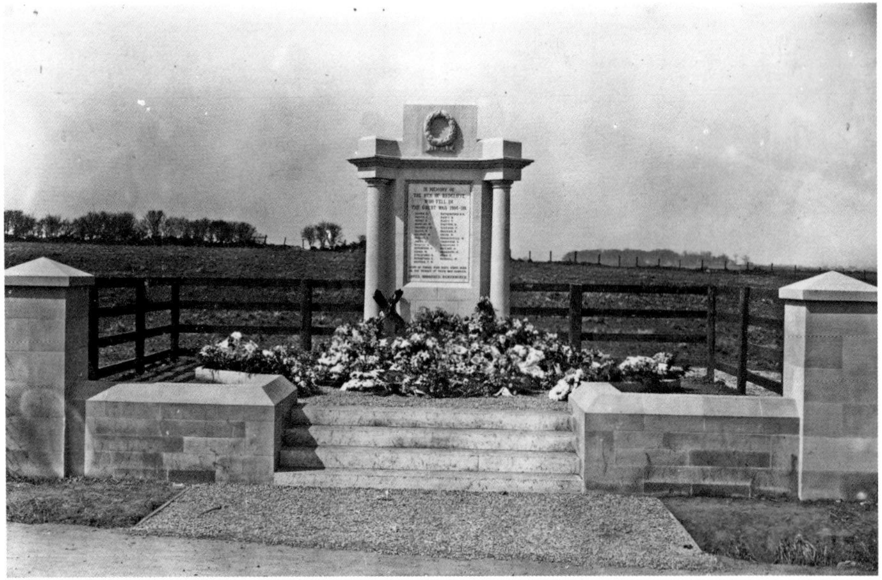

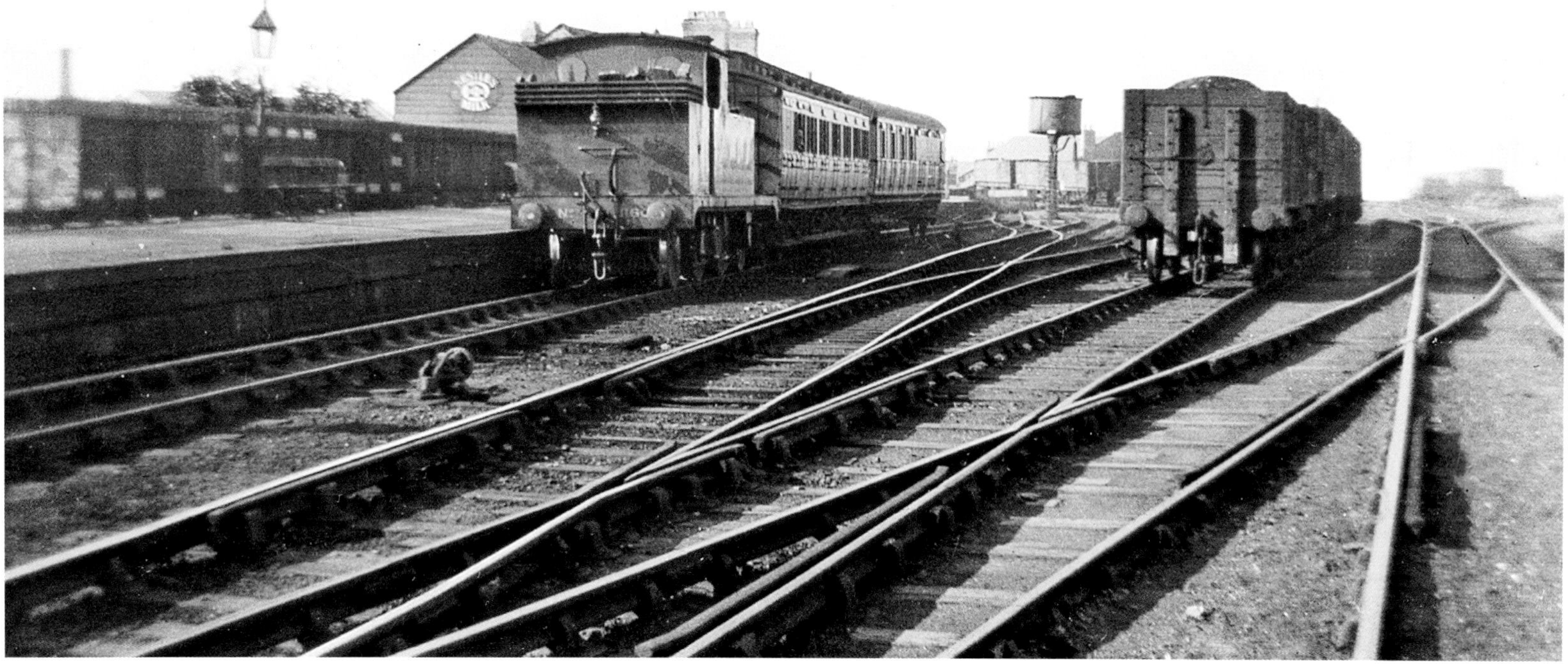

The Amble branch railway line was opened in September 1849. It left the main east coast line about a mile north of Chevington at Amble Junction – the destination of the branch was usually used to name the junction. For thirty years the line was only used for freight, but in June 1879 a station was opened at Amble and a passenger service introduced that continued until July 1930. This picture, believed to date from 1930, shows the station with the little tank engine and carriages that shuttled back and forth along the six miles between Amble and Chevington, where passengers could change trains for more distant destinations. There were a couple of variations to this regular pattern of services on Saturdays, with one train running through to Morpeth and a late night train for revellers between Amble and the only intermediate station on the line at Broomhill. There was no service on Sundays. The last passenger train to visit Amble was an enthusiasts' special in 1963, a few years before the line closed.

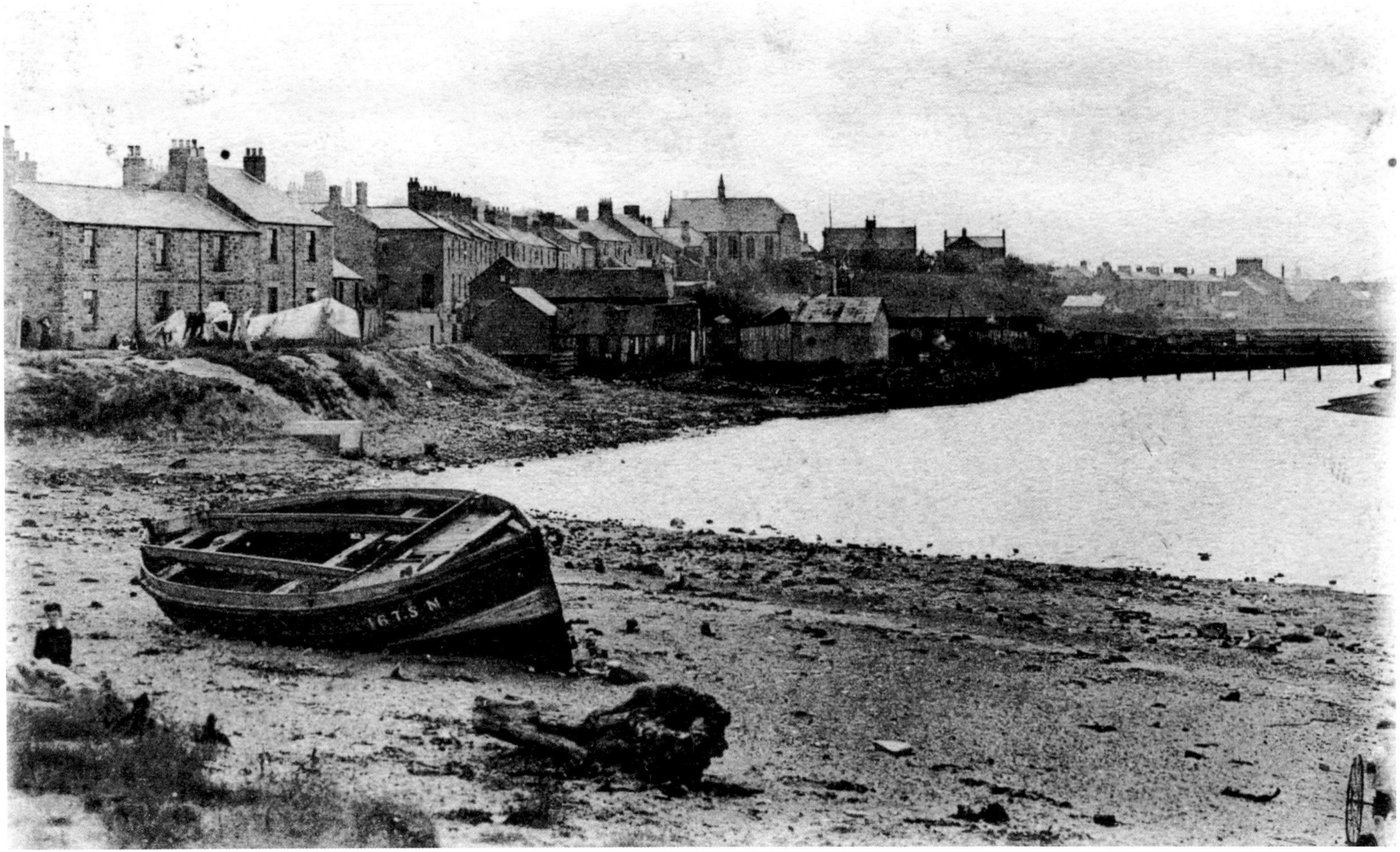

As the River Coquet flowed past the town it was joined by the Guilders Burn, which at its mouth, the Gut, widened into a bay. The area around the bay, known as the dinghy's shore, was used to beach small fishing boats, like the one in this picture – a reminder that as well as exporting coal Amble has a fishing tradition. Painted on the boat's bow is a registration number, which, if the British White Herring Act of 1860 was strictly adhered to, had to be painted in white on a black background. The letters indicate the port of registry and were often made up of the town's first and last letters like BK for Berwick or BH for Blyth, but this little boat sports the more unusual SN for Shields North. There was no fishing boat registry for Amble itself. Central amongst the cluster of buildings in the background of the picture is the Wesleyan Methodist Church in High Street.

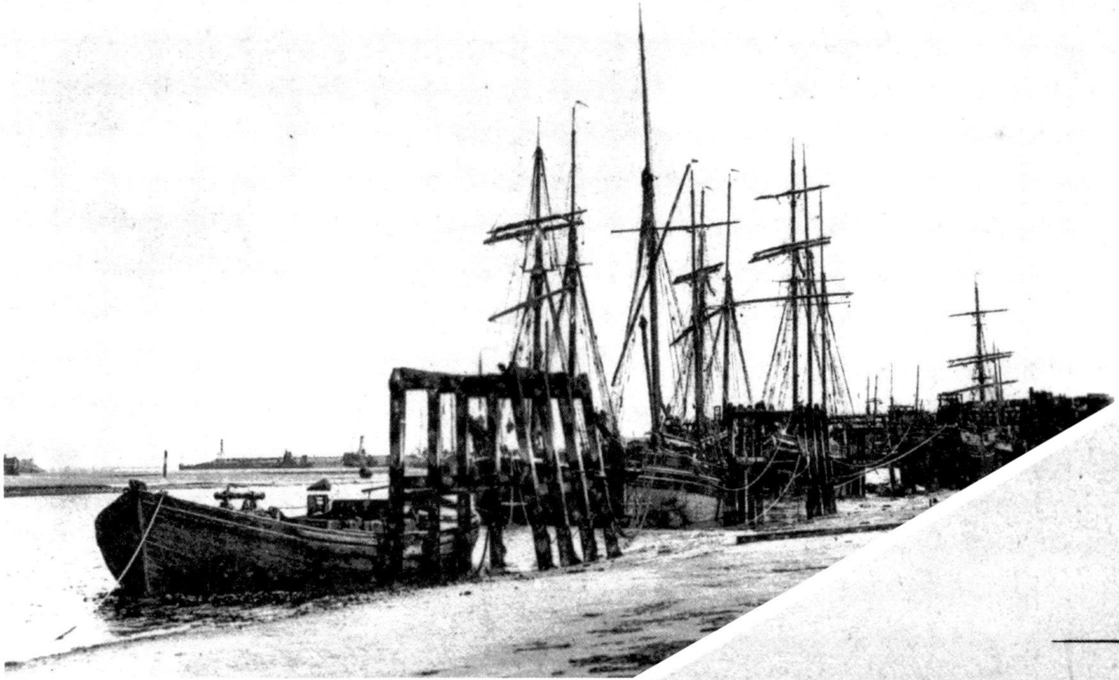

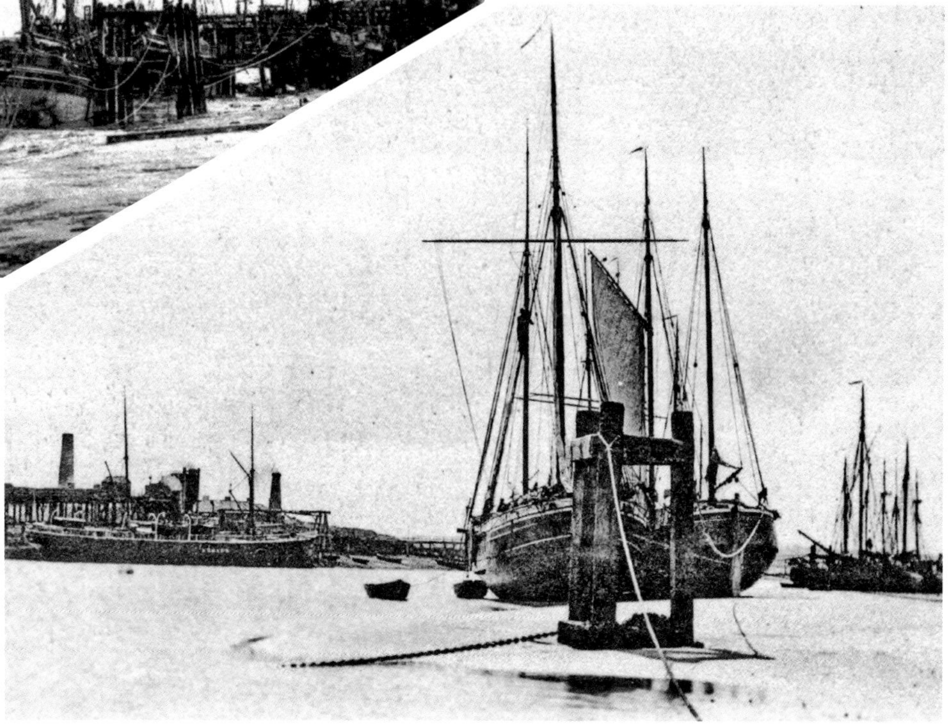

There was one reason for building the Amble branch railway, and that was to get coal to the harbour, seen here in pictures from the late nineteenth century. The trade began to develop in the 1830s when railways were in their infancy and the tried and trusted method of moving coal was to get it by wagon-way to the nearest point where it could be loaded onto boats or barges. The problem faced by the coal owners was that the Coquet was ill suited for shipping, so they drew up plans and in 1837 persuaded parliament to pass the Warkworth Harbour Act, authorising the appointment of harbour commissioners to develop the port. More plans were produced and different engineers consulted until John Rennie was engaged to oversee the work. When construction began in 1838, the little town of Amble also began to grow, but by that time the Warkworth Harbour name was fixed.

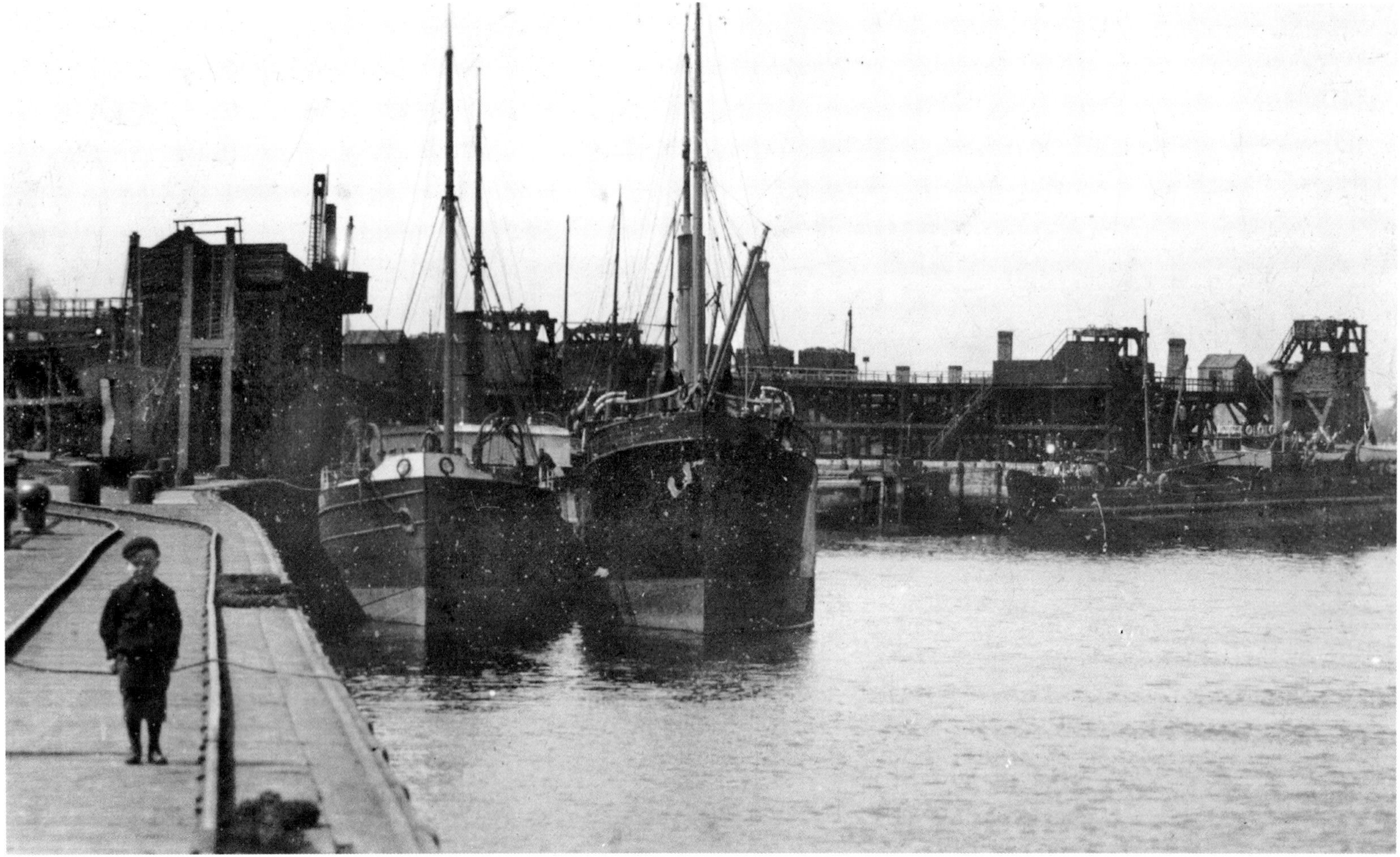

Taming a tidal river at the point where it enters the sea was never going to be easy, but the job was made more difficult by a complicated and ultimately unsatisfactory contractual arrangement with one of the coal lessees. It didn't help either that storm damage to the North Pier resulted in substantial reconstruction, so that a job that should have been completed in 1842 was not signed off by John Rennie until 1849. By that time the works had cost much more than expected and revenues from coal shipments were insufficient to justify the expense. The finances remained precarious for the next twenty years until a new consulting engineer, Thomas Meik, was brought in. His incremental approach to improvements made the port suitable for larger ships and finally able to realise its full potential. It is seen here with a little boy happily tempting providence by standing between the rails on the quayside.

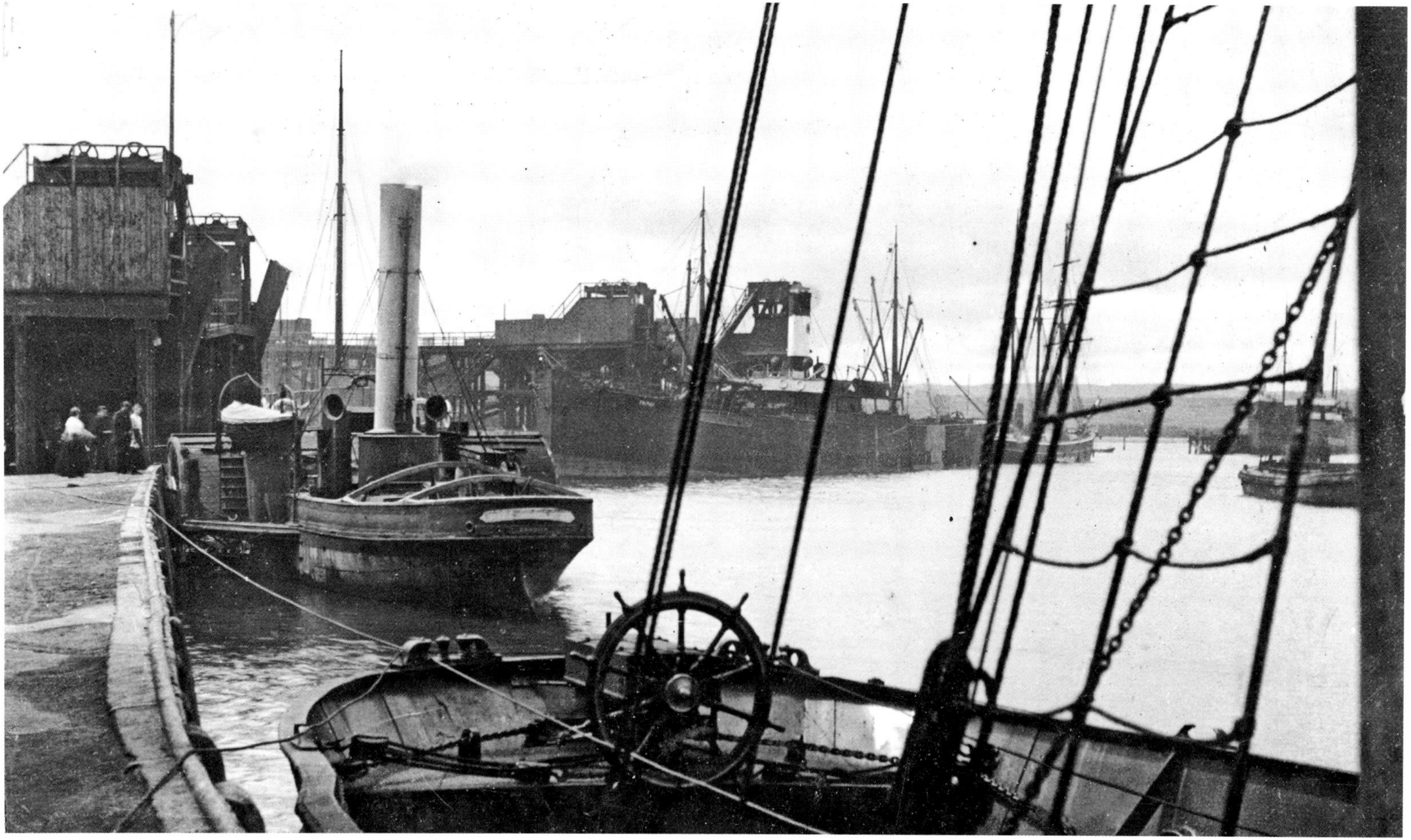

The railways from the branch line and the collieries terminated at large structures known as staithes. These were designed to tip up railway trucks, to empty their load of coal down a chute into the holds of ships, and in the process create a cloud of black dust that covered everything - something your scribe can testify to having been in the hold of a small ship when a truckload of coal was tipped into it. A team of men known as trimmers had the job of spreading the coal in the ship's hold to ensure it was evenly distributed. Amble's fortunes were to some extent constrained by the number of pits feeding coal into it. There were two principal operations, both were developed in the 1830s and 1840s and gave their names to Amble's quays: Broomhill, in the foreground of this picture and Radcliffe beyond, but in this picture the Broomhill staithes are empty, with a paddle tug tied up alongside. These little boats were needed to help the single screw coal ships manoeuvre in the confines of the harbour.

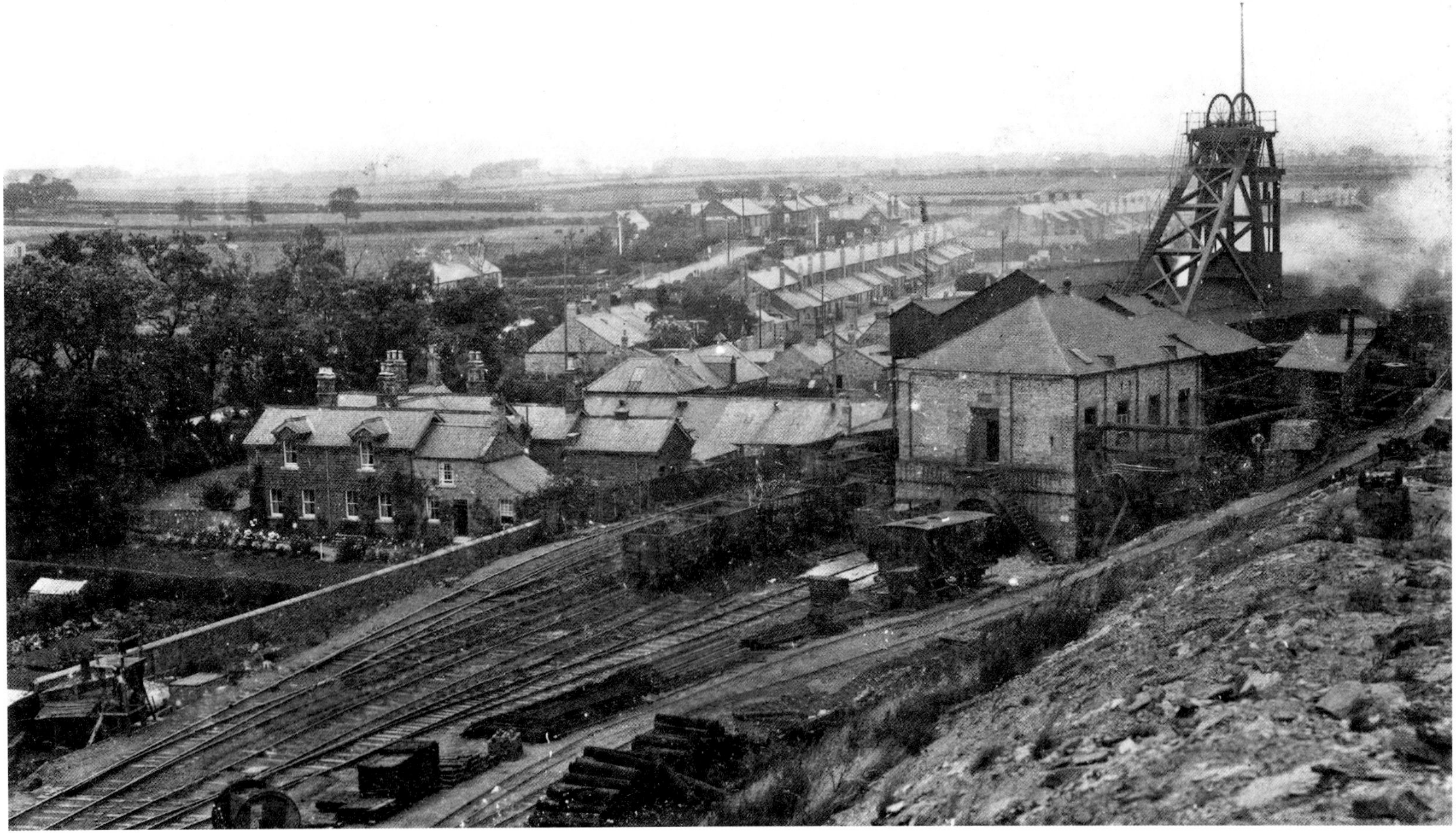

Of the two main colliery groups, Broomhill, seen here with its adjacent village, was marginally the younger. Sinking began in 1849 and an additional shaft was sunk in 1866. The colliery worked steam and household coals from seams with names like Queen, Albert, Beaumont, Main and Givens until closure in 1961. Togston Colliery, adjacent to Broomhill, worked the same field and there were other nearby collieries at Chevington Drift and Chevington. Radcliffe was closed in the 1890s due to faulting, but newer developments at Newburgh and Hauxley ensured that the field of good steam coal continued to be exploited. A by-product from all of the pits was clay – coal is the compressed remains of ancient trees that grew in primeval swamps, the muddy swamp beds formed the rock-hard clay found in coalmines. It was delivered to a brick works at Amble – the chimneys can be seen in the backgrounds of pictures on pages 29 and 30 – which produced bricks with the brand name of Radcliffe.

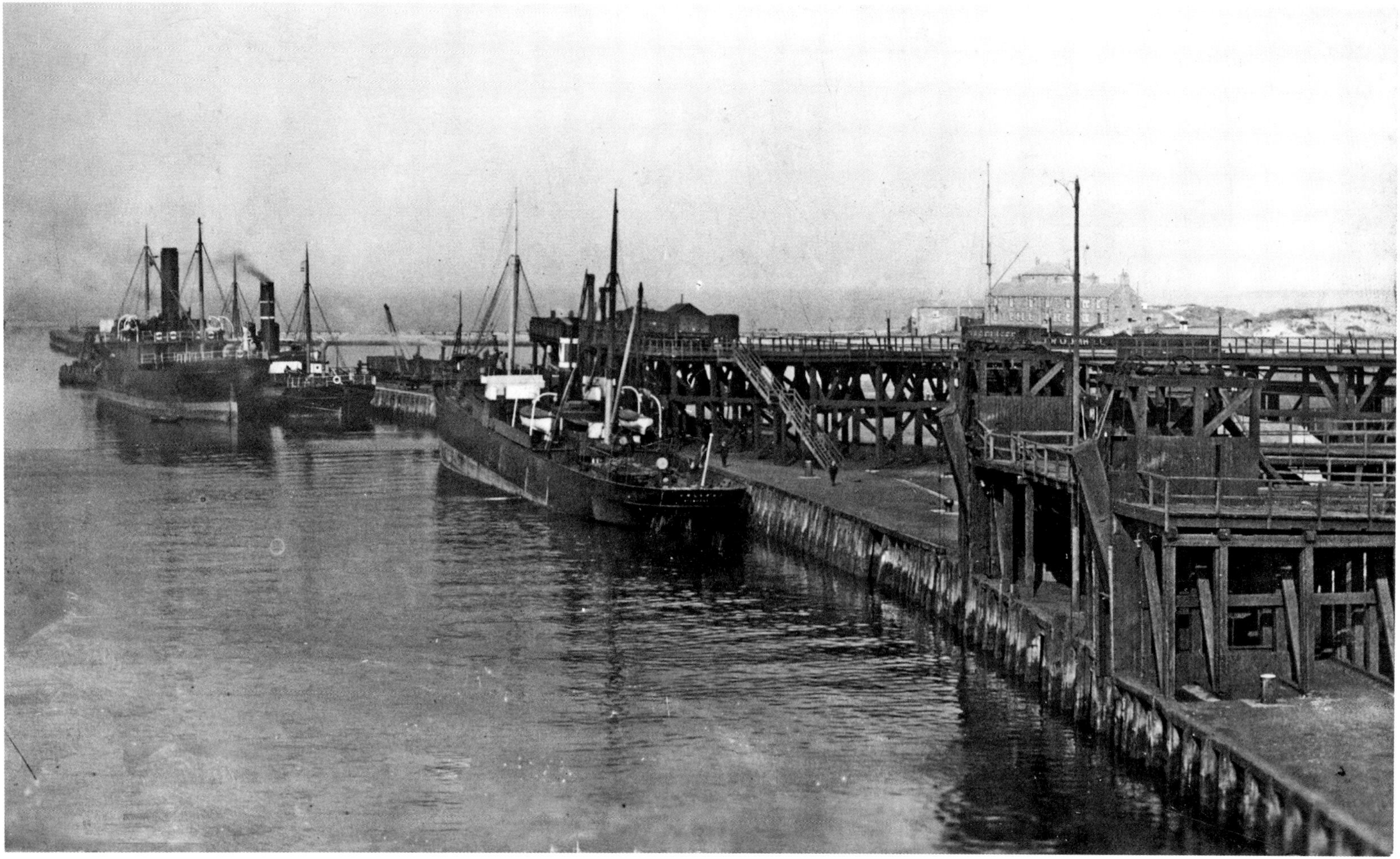

Cargoes of coal left Amble on ships bound for ports throughout Britain and Europe and some of these unglamorous vessels are seen here at the Broomhill quay staithes. The ship closest to camera appears to have had her after holds filled and been moved so that coal can be loaded into the forward holds. It is in the nature of extractive industries that, at some stage, the mineral will run out and the last of the local coal workings at Hauxley closed in 1966. Prior to that Amble had attracted another customer, the Co-operative Wholesale Society (CWS) who acquired Langdale Pit, near Alnwick, in 1917 and redeveloped it as Shilbottle Colliery, its good household coal finding markets up and down the east coast. With the collieries closing, the staithes were left idle. They ceased working in the late 1960s and shortly afterwards the railway tracks were lifted and the infrastructure that had given Amble life was demolished.

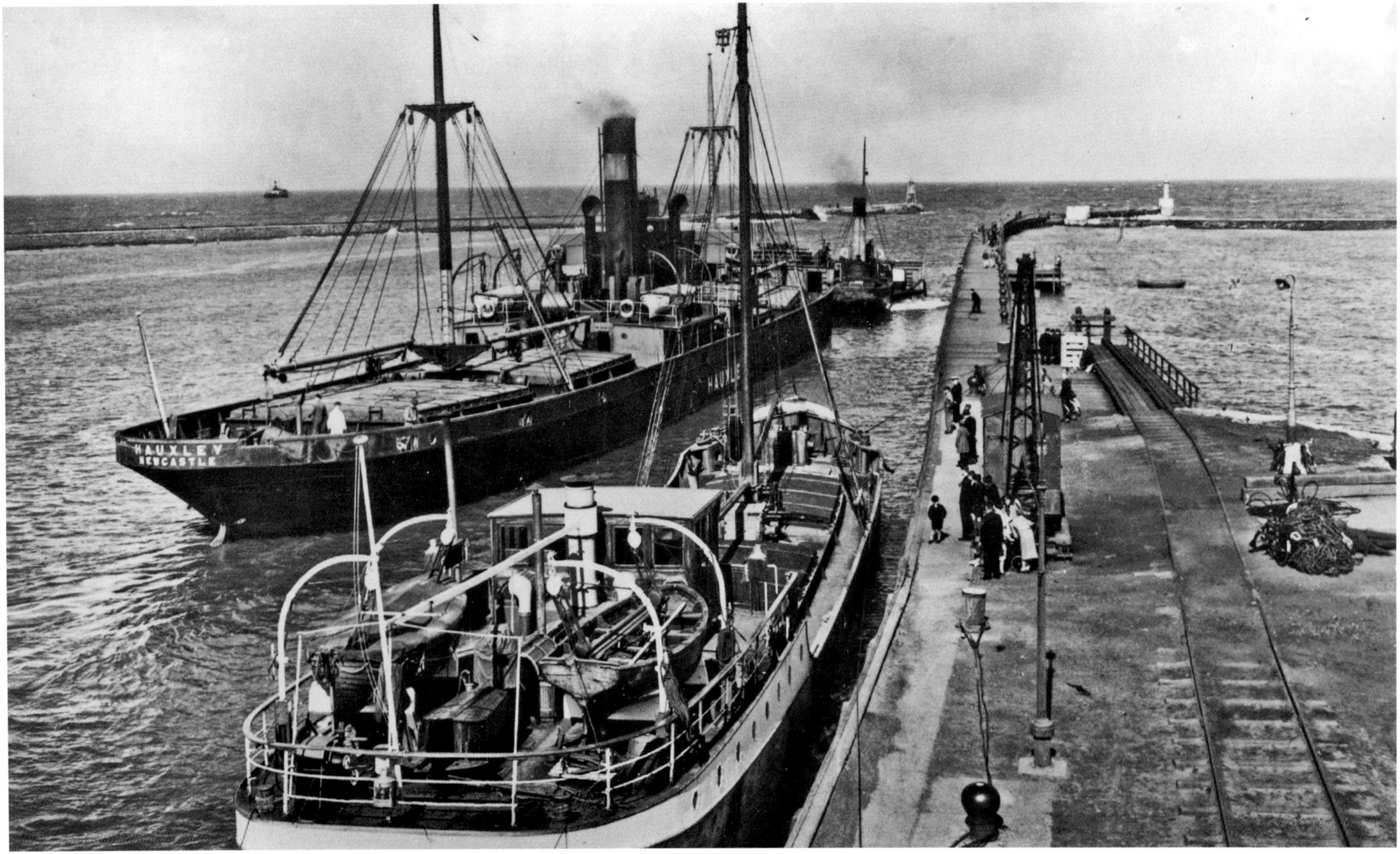

The *Hauxley*, seen here at the harbour mouth, was typical of the kind of ship able to work in and out of the harbour. Built in 1925 by the Furness Shipbuilding Company of Middlesbrough, she weighed 1,595 tons, was 246 feet long, 39 feet in the beam and drew 19 feet of water – close to the limit for getting in and out of Amble. She was initially one of a small fleet of colliers that all bore local names and were owned by Broomhill Collieries, but from 1936 the ships were operated by a subsidiary company, Broomhill Steamships Ltd. She was in their ownership when this picture was taken in 1938. A couple of years later, in October 1940 and with the country at war, *Hauxley* was in a convoy heading north from London for another cargo of coal when she was torpedoed and sank. Curiously, this picture was used as a postcard in the early 1950s more than a decade after the ship had been sunk by enemy action.

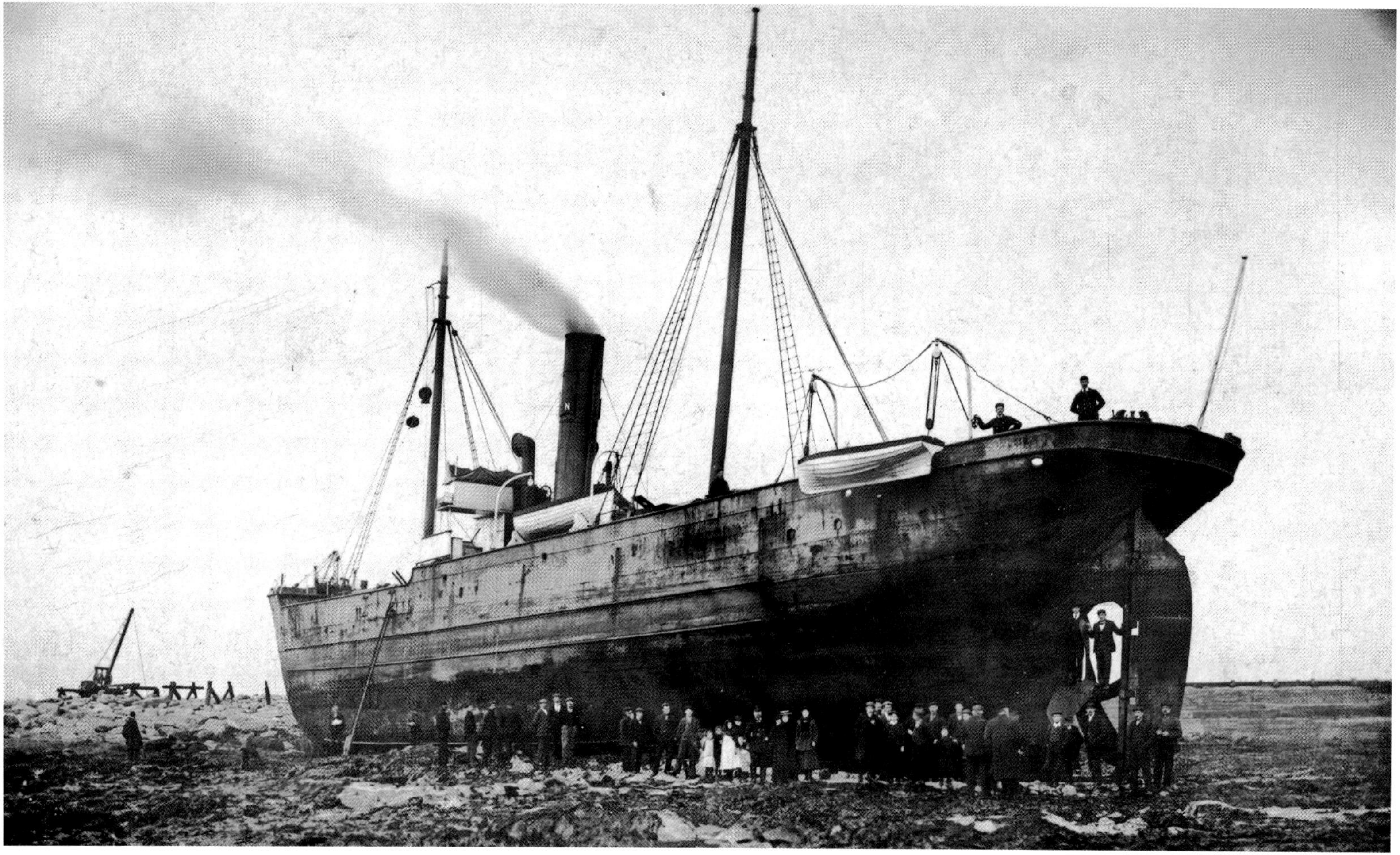

Zealandia was another ship that was typical of the type that used the port, although untypically she ended her voyage from Ghent, at the end of October 1905, by ploughing straight onto the rocks beside Cliff House. There was speculation that, in poor visibility and without bothering to engage a pilot, her skipper mistook the light on the South Pier for the North and drove hard and straight to the wrong side of it. It was two hours before high tide, so the boat landed a long way up the shore and was left high and dry when the tide went out. Shore based rescuers were able to get a line aboard to rescue the crew, but the harbour tugs were also able to come alongside and they took the men off. A couple of weeks later a sailing vessel known as the *Maria Stella* landed on the shore beside the stricken ship, but while she was re-floated, the *Zealandia* was broken up for scrap.

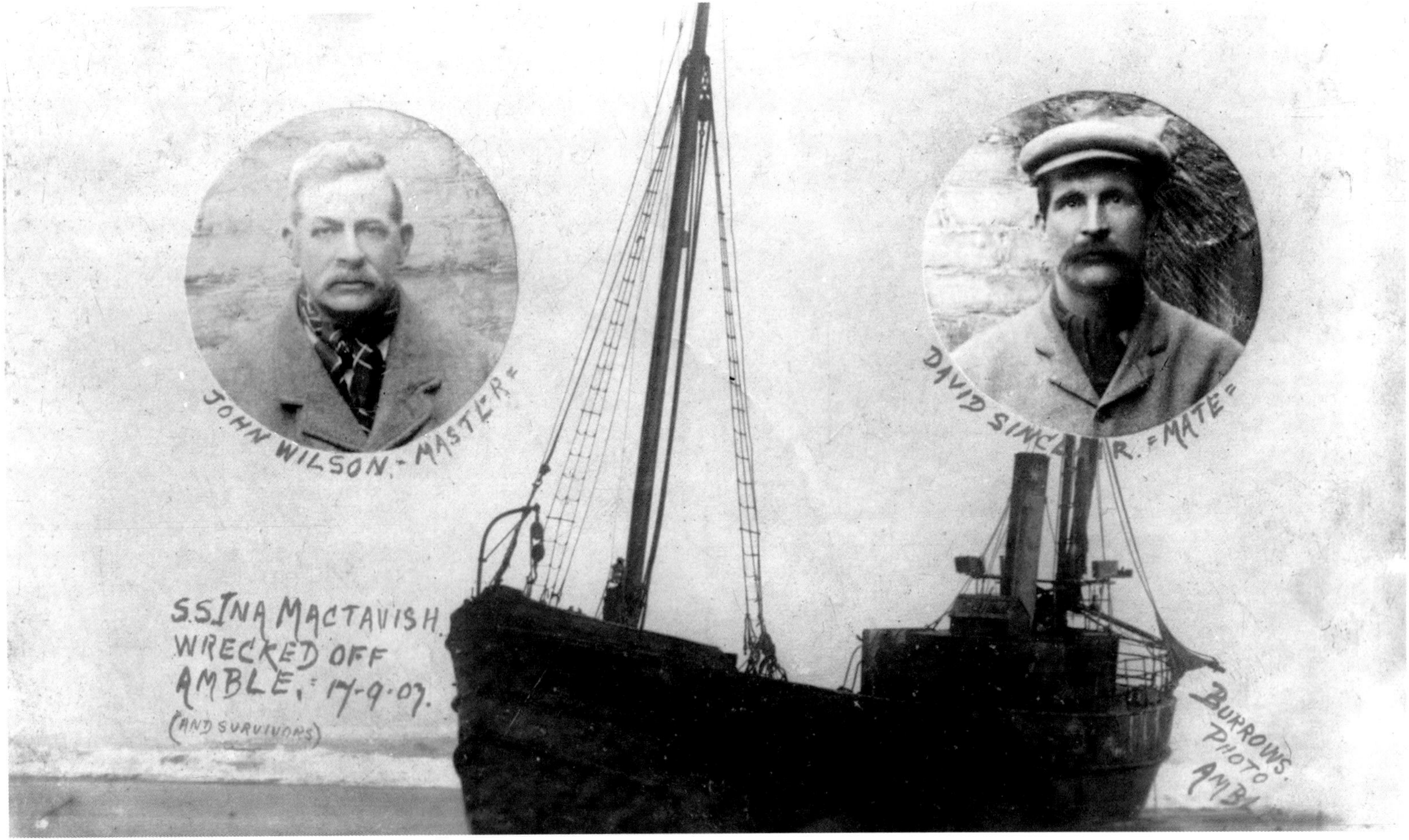

The steam lighter *Ina Mactavish* was built in 1886 at a boatyard on the Forth & Clyde Canal in Glasgow and worked the Clyde estuary until she sank in 1906. Raised, repaired and lengthened, she was bought by owner/skipper John Wilson of Leith. He left South Shields with a cargo of lime for Aberdeen on 16th October 1907, but at about ten o'clock that night, the ship's condenser broke down. John Wilson was able to keep going ahead until the engine stopped about eight hours later. With the aid of a lugsail, the skipper steered for the shore and grounded just to the south of the Birling Carrs at about nine o'clock on the morning of 17th October (the picture has been incorrectly dated. Coastguard teams from Amble and Alnmouth rushed to set up their rocket apparatus, but were unable to get a rope aboard the stricken vessel. The four men on board were exhausted, and having failed to secure a line to the shore, had no option but to wait for rescue. They tried to lash themselves to the rigging, but the engineer was washed overboard and drowned.

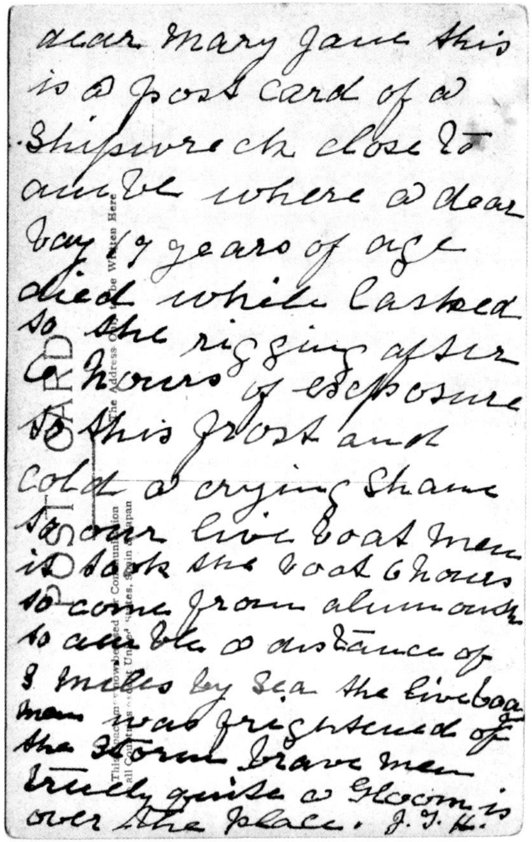
dear Mary Jane this
is a post card of a
Shipwreck close to
amble where a dear
boy 17 years of age
died while lashed
to the rigging after
6 hours of exposure
to this frost and
cold a crying Shame
to our live boat men
it took the boat 6 hours
to come from alnmouth
to amble a distance of
3 miles by sea the liveboat
men was frightened of
the storm brave men
truely quite a Gloom is
over the place. J.T.H.

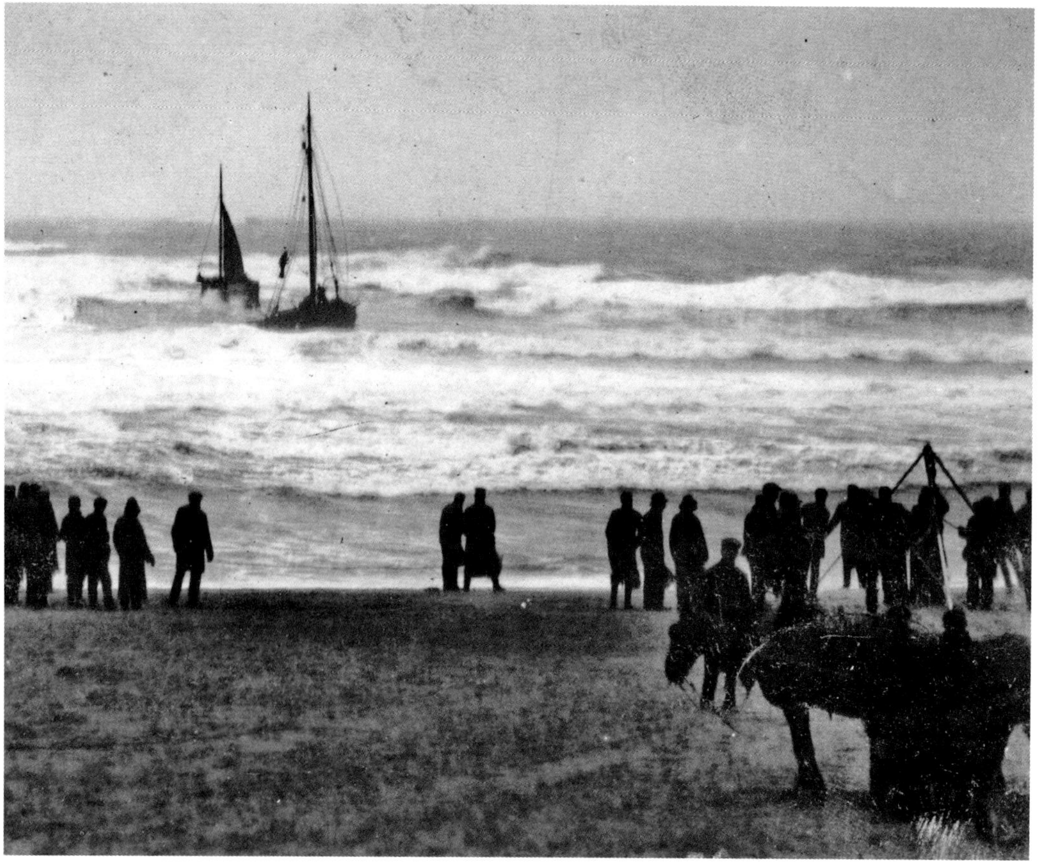

Three miles away in Alnmouth, dithering and confusion delayed the lifeboat, which failed to appear until six hours after the *Ina Mactavish* had gone aground and half an hour after the 17 year-old cook died. The skipper and his mate were saved, and in an extraordinary act of bravery, Police Sergeant Andrew Barton and coastguard boatman Peter Holbert swam out to recover the cook's body. The ship was later re-floated: a loose nut had caused the condenser problem and a rope, washed overboard, had fouled the propeller, stopping the engine. At the subsequent inquiry, the skipper was commended for his seamanship, but faulted for not sending up a distress flare as soon as the engine stopped. Criticism of the RNLI echoed the sentiments expressed in this contemporary account written on the back of a postcard by a woman from Amble.

"Dear Mary Jane, this is a post card of a shipwreck close to Amble where a dear boy, 17 years of age, died while lashed to the rigging after six hours of exposure to this frost and cold – a crying shame to our lifeboat men, it took the boat six hours to come from Alnmouth to Amble, a distance of three miles by sea. The lifeboat men were frightened of the storm, brave men. Truly quite a gloom is over the place. J.T.H."

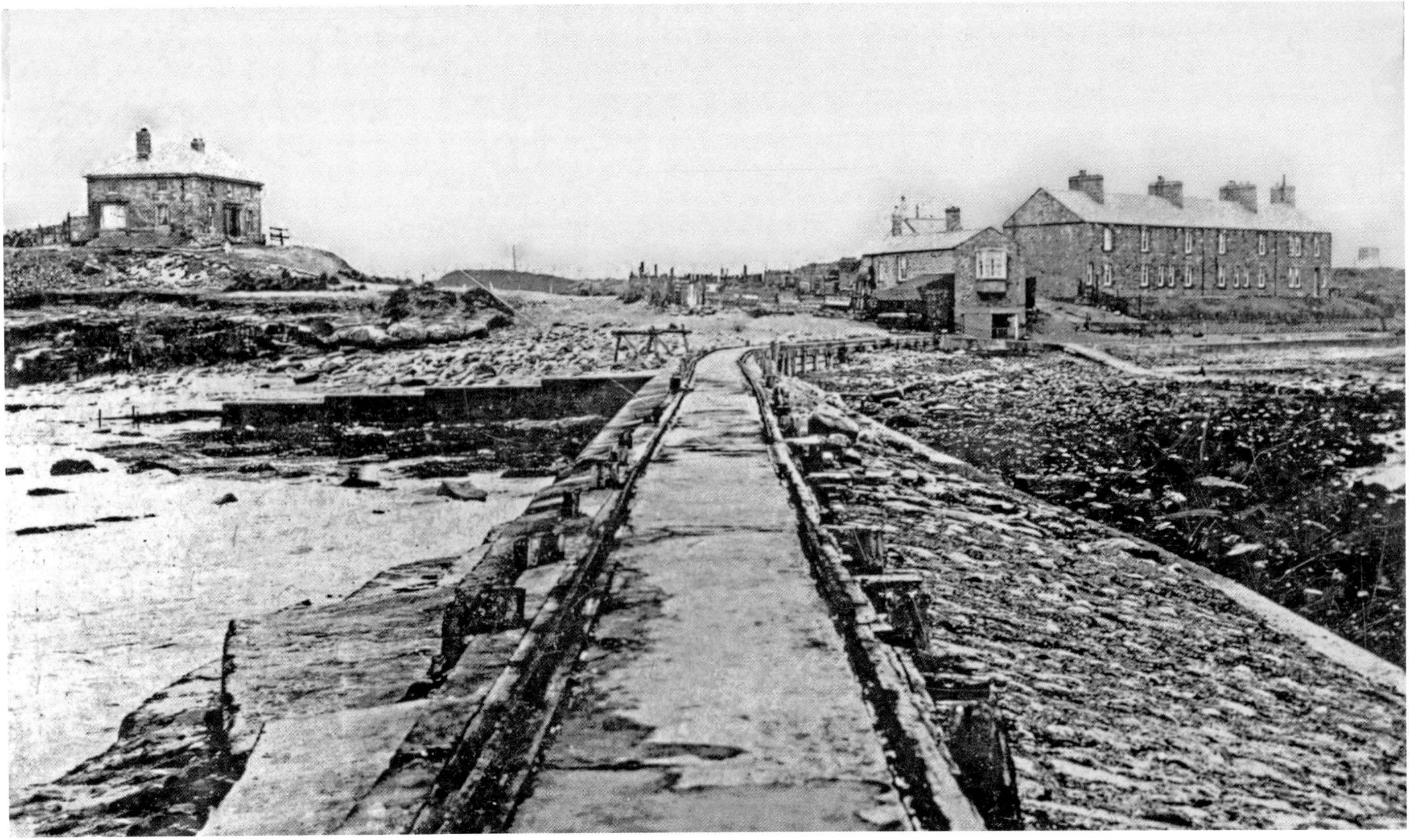

It was (indeed still is) the coastguard's role to react to potential or actual maritime incidents, like that of the *Ina Mactavish*. Described at the time as the 'aye ready' men, the coastguard teams, in trying to get a line aboard the stricken vessel, did everything they could to lessen that unfolding tragedy. They were based in these buildings at the end of the breakwater linking the South Pier to the shore. The buildings on the right were the coastguard cottages; the coastguard station was the large building on the left. Known as Cliff House, it had originally been built by the contractors for the harbour works as a base for their site manager. It also catered for the spiritual and earthly needs of their employees by incorporating a room for worship and a truck shop, also known as a tommy shop, where workers could be paid in kind, rather than cash. Such company stores were common in isolated industrial communities, but not popular.

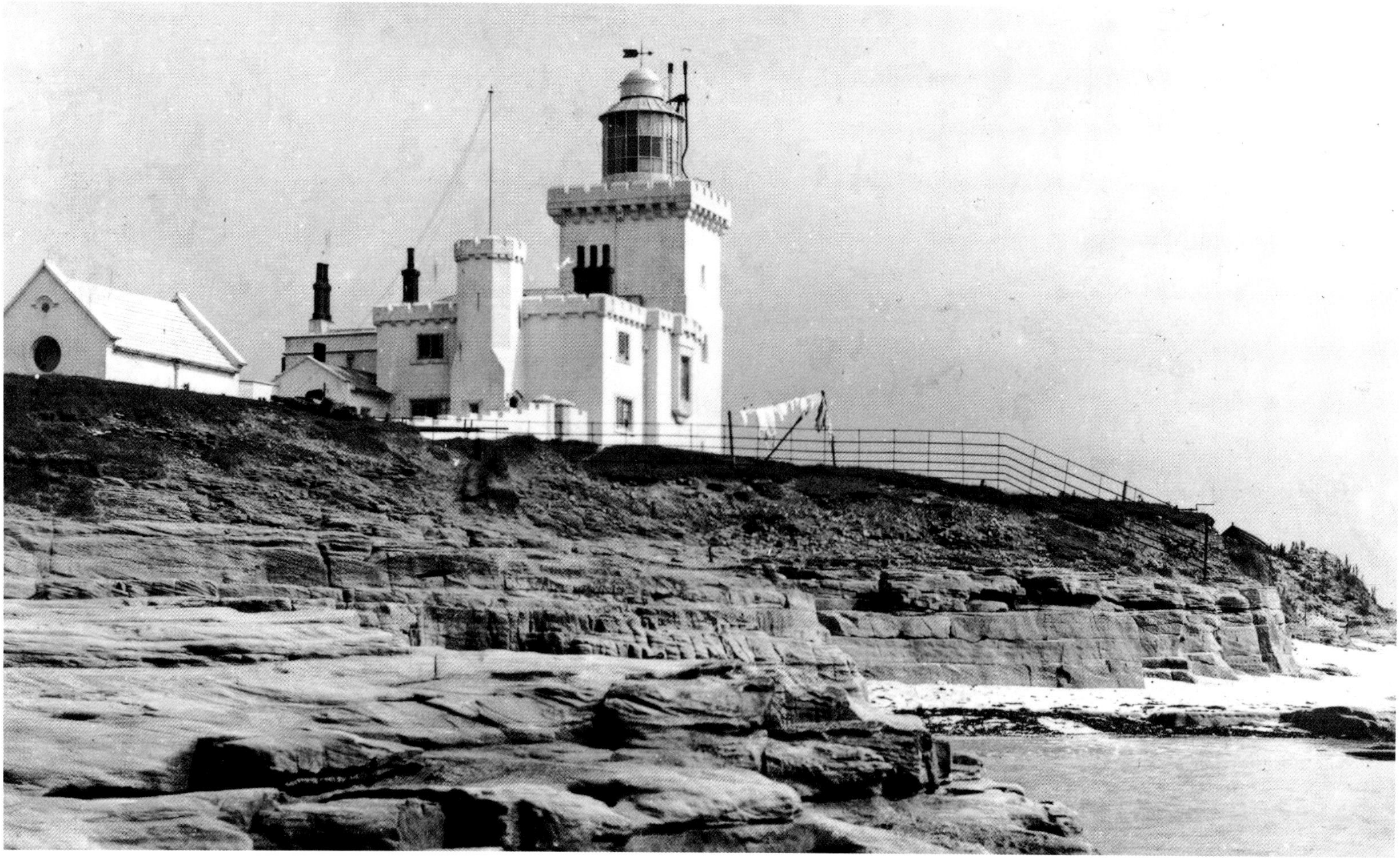

Situated a mile and a bit off the river mouth, Coquet Island was in the past a refuge for monks and in the present is a sanctuary for birds. At the start of the 1840s it was also in a critical position for shipping moving up and down the east coast, but especially for vessels intending to swing in to the developing Warkworth Harbour at Amble. Trinity House, the authority charged with providing navigational aids, set about erecting a lighthouse on the island. Built to the designs of James Walker, it was a square tower, 24 feet high, completed in 1841 and lit for the first time in October of that year. The first keeper, William Darling, was the brother of Grace Darling, who famously helped her father, also William, keeper of the Longstone Lighthouse on the Farne Islands, to rescue survivors from the wreck of the *Forfarshire* in 1838.

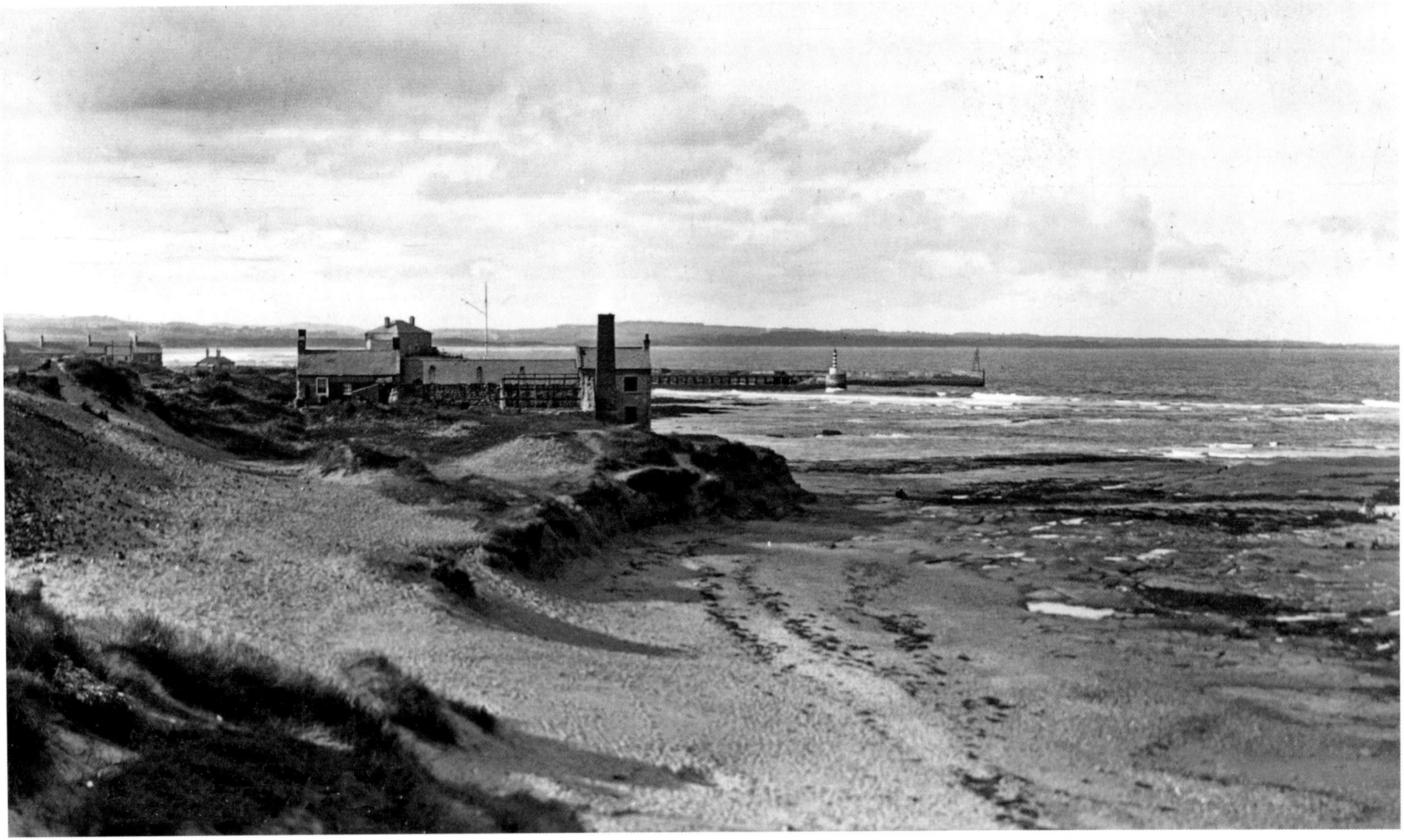

The buildings in this view of the beach were originally associated with a salt industry that is known to have been in existence in the early seventeenth century, predating Amble by over 200 years. In those early days salt was essential for the preservation of food and especially in this locality, fish. Coal and seawater were needed to make salt; it took about sixteen tons of coal to make one ton of salt. Salt pans were typically iron trays approximately six yards long by three yards wide and eighteen inches deep. Set on brick or stone pillars, so they could be fired underneath, they were located in pan houses, simple shed-like structures with a chimney or a hole in the roof to let out the smoke and steam. When the salt tax was reduced in 1823 and then repealed in 1825, coastal works struggled to compete with large operations like those in Cheshire, but Amble's works defied the odds for some time. Since the closure of the works, these cottages have become known as Island View.

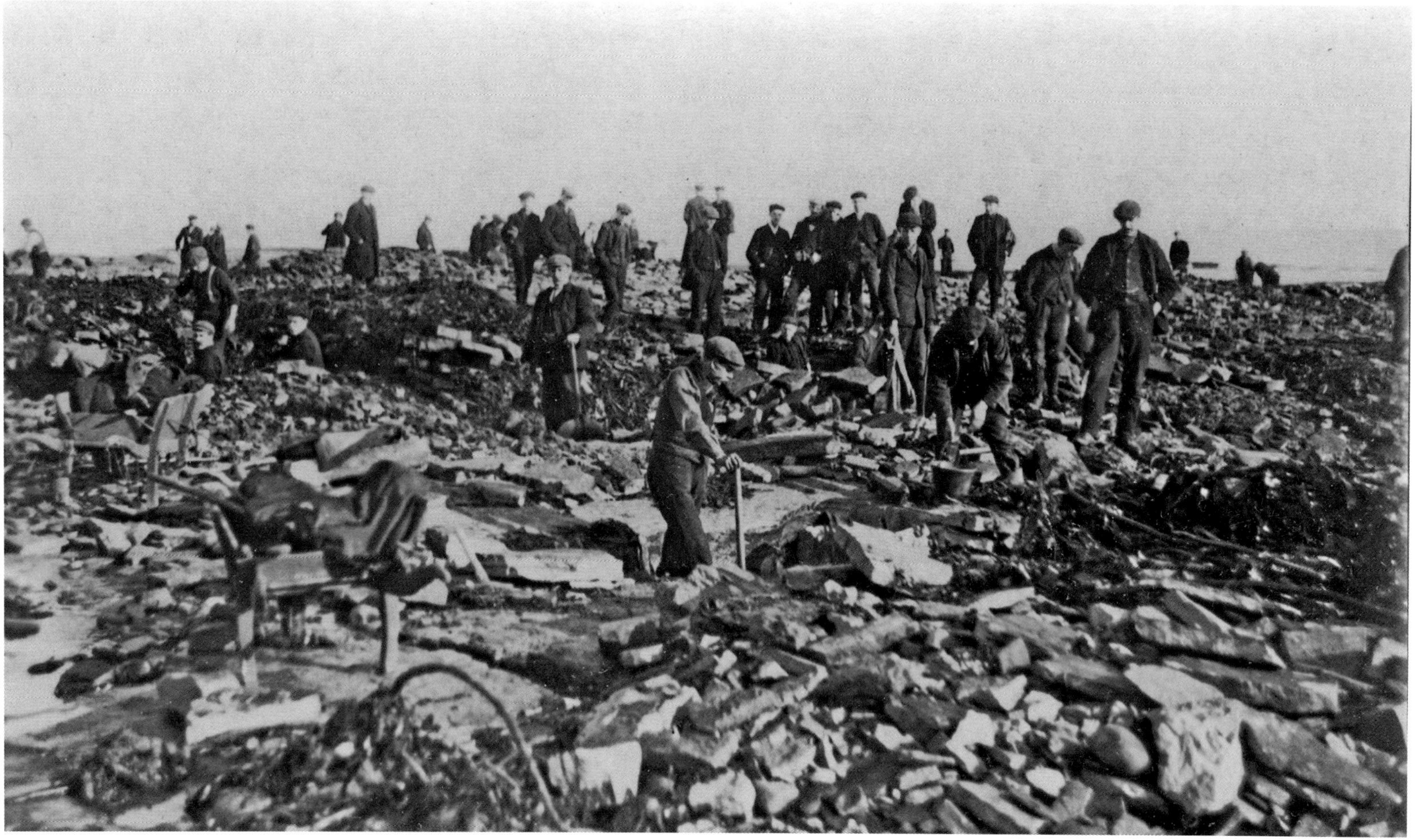

Entitled 'Coal Hewing on Amble Beach' this undated picture, and the one on the front cover, shows men apparently digging into outcropping seams of coal. They have attracted a number of onlookers, and cameras, which suggests that this was unusual, as if the outcrop had just been exposed, or this was happening during a strike or some other time of fuel shortage. These coal seams were on the edge of the great Northumberland and Durham coalfield, an area that, on a map, looks like a pyramid with the base near Tees-side and the apex at Amble. The coal measures dipped in the west, were largely flat in the east, rose to surface at places near the coast and extended well out beyond the shoreline, under the sea. There were some sixty seams of coal, over twenty of which could be worked by deep mining. The coals ranged from high quality coking and gas coal in the south to excellent steam and household coal near Amble. That will have been a valuable prize for these beach miners.

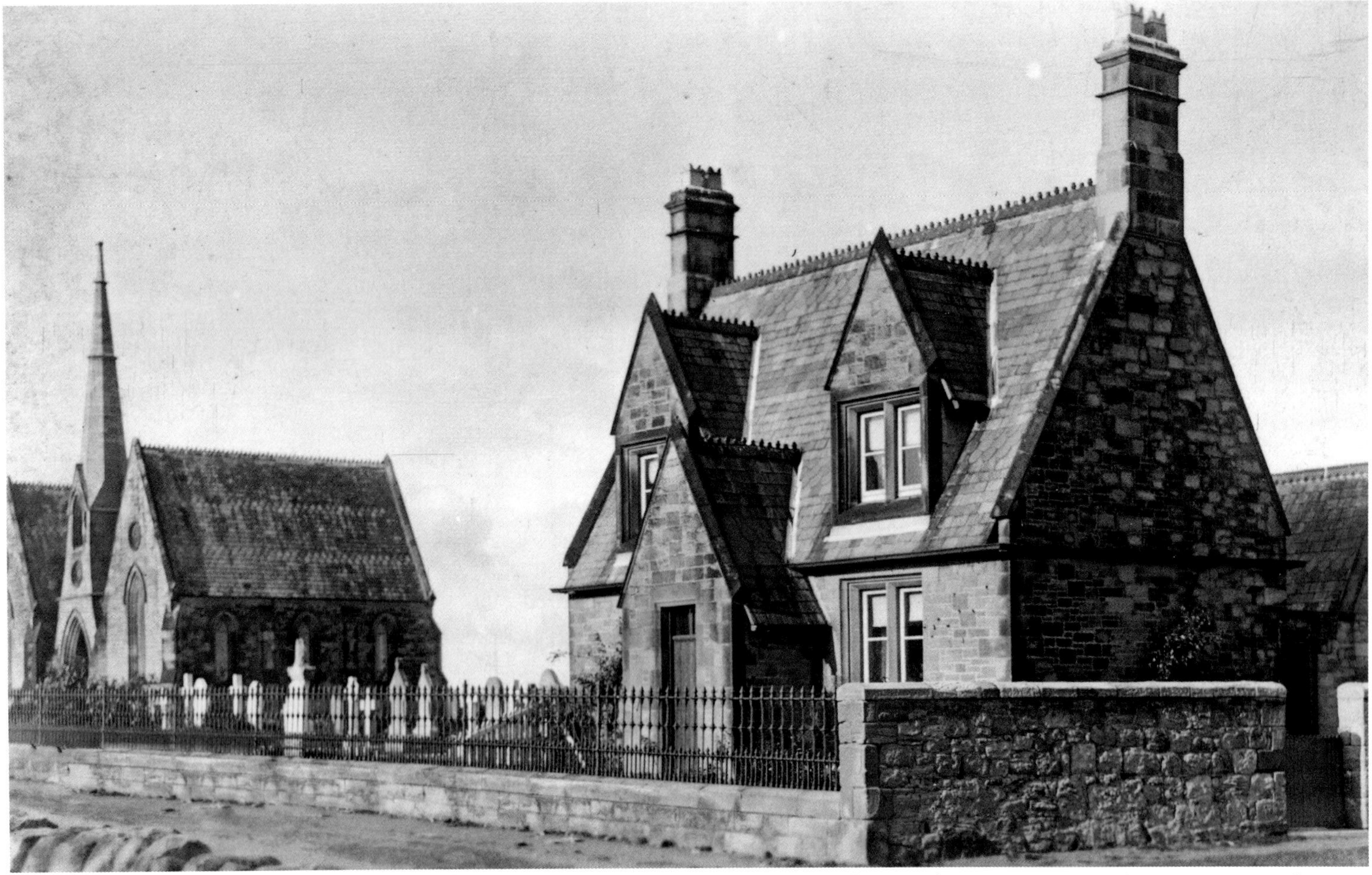

The practice of interring deceased townspeople in Warkworth had become unsustainable by the time that Amble was made a separate parish in 1869. To resolve the situation, a burial board was set up which procured a two-and-half acre site on the links for a cemetery. Plans were drawn up for an attendant's house, boundary walls and an entrance arch with spire and flanking chapels. The foundation stone for the chapels was laid in July 1877 and the cemetery was consecrated in April the following year. Two roughly equal portions were set aside for Church of England and non-conformist believers, and smaller sections were allocated to Catholics and people who did not want a Christian burial. The cemetery was soon found to be inadequate and so a new one, on an eleven acre site, was opened in 1905. It became known as the West Cemetery and the old one the East Cemetery. It is seen here at about that time. The two chapels at the entrance were demolished in 1971, but the distinctive spire remained as a local landmark.

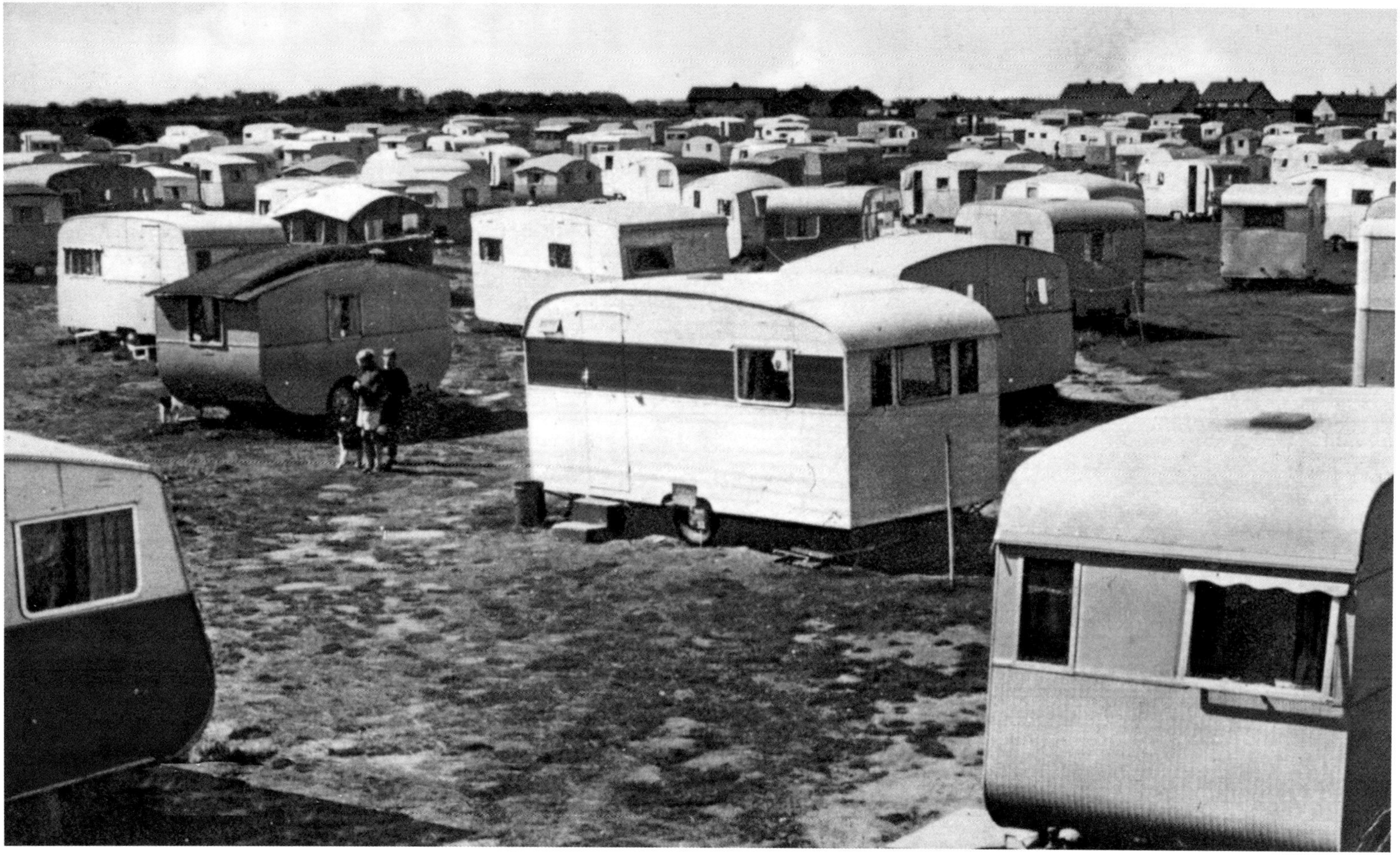

People had been parking caravans among the dunes for some time before 1964 when the Amble Urban District Council purchased Links Farm and established a caravan park. As this postcard shows, the site lacked sophistication, but if the message on the back is any guide, the people who came were determined to enjoy themselves. Implying that they were in the Bahamas the writers refer to ripe coconuts and drinks on ice before shattering the illusion by scoffing at Seahouses and bemoaning the failure of the Beatles to turn up for their booking at the club. Caravans on the site, and especially those on the dunes, were badly damaged in a fierce storm in January 1968, when thirty were wrecked and another fifty blown over. Since then, the site has become privately owned and gone up-market with spacious holiday homes and on-site facilities like a gym, sauna, swimming pool, café and children's play area.

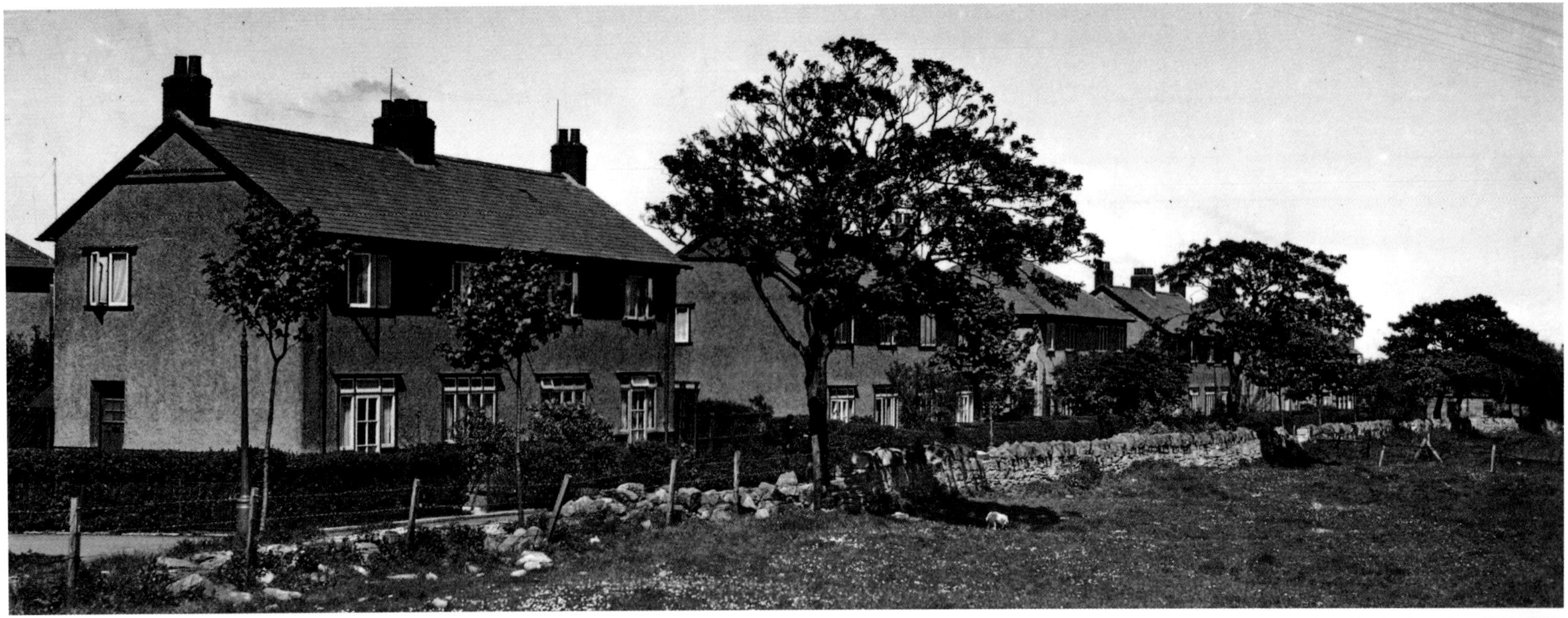

Nineteenth century Amble wasn't entirely confined by the river and railway. Gloster Hill was a separate, if scarcely detached, entity to the west and bridges allowed the town to spread beyond the tracks, but it remained a tight little community. That changed after the First World War, although the national desire to create 'homes fit for heroes' was slow to manifest itself in actual buildings. Nevertheless Amble did start to expand in the 1920s and 30s as houses like these in Central Avenue and South Avenue were built. This expansion westward was matched in the east with development spreading across the links towards the East Cemetery. Housing was also built to accommodate people displaced from Radcliffe when the village was demolished in 1971, with street names taken from the old village.

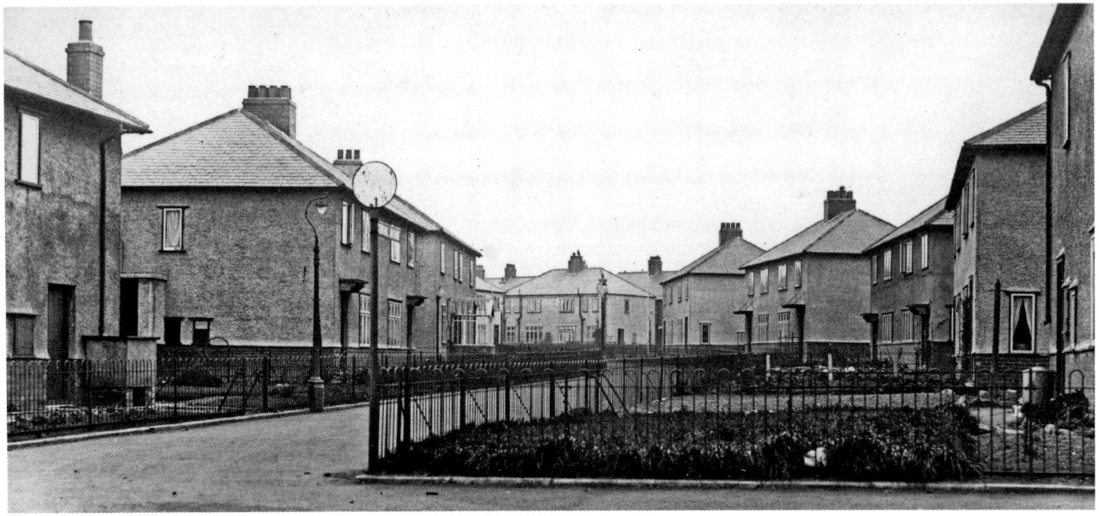

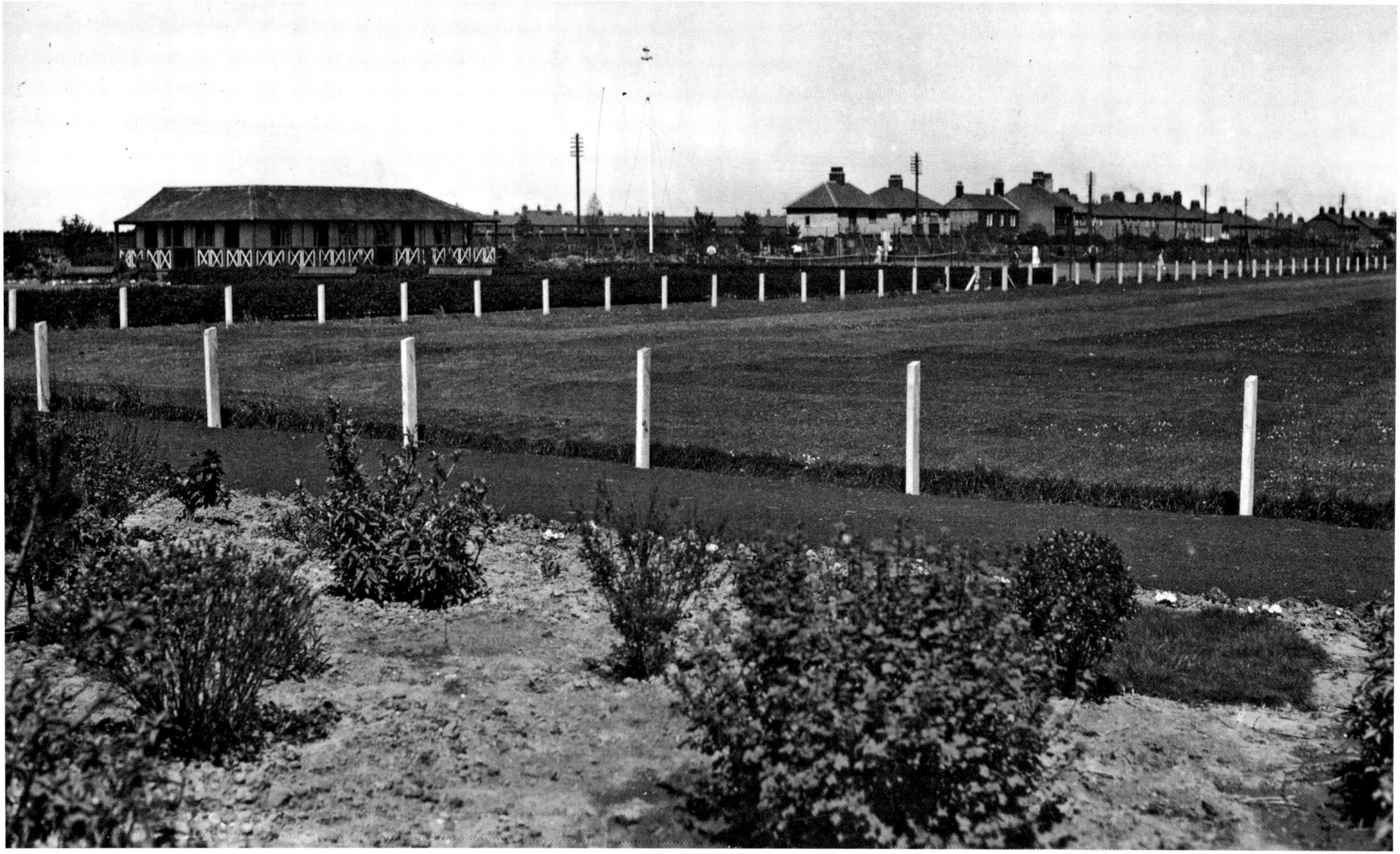

The 1920s is usually regarded as a time of strife in the coal industry, but there was one positive development, the establishment of the Miner's Welfare Fund in 1920. It was raised with contributions from mine workers and the owners who paid a levy of a penny on every ton of coal, and this was extended in 1926 to pay for pithead baths. The fund was administered by local committees, which were drawn from both management and unions, so that the money was spent the way people wanted. It paid for institutes, convalescent homes and recreational facilities like Welfare Park, a former cricket field taken over by the welfare committee in the 1930s. Acklington Road is seen behind the park with South Avenue in the distance. Welfare Park hosted many sporting activities, although football matches were the most popular with one attracting a crowd of around 2,000 people. The park has since fallen on hard times.

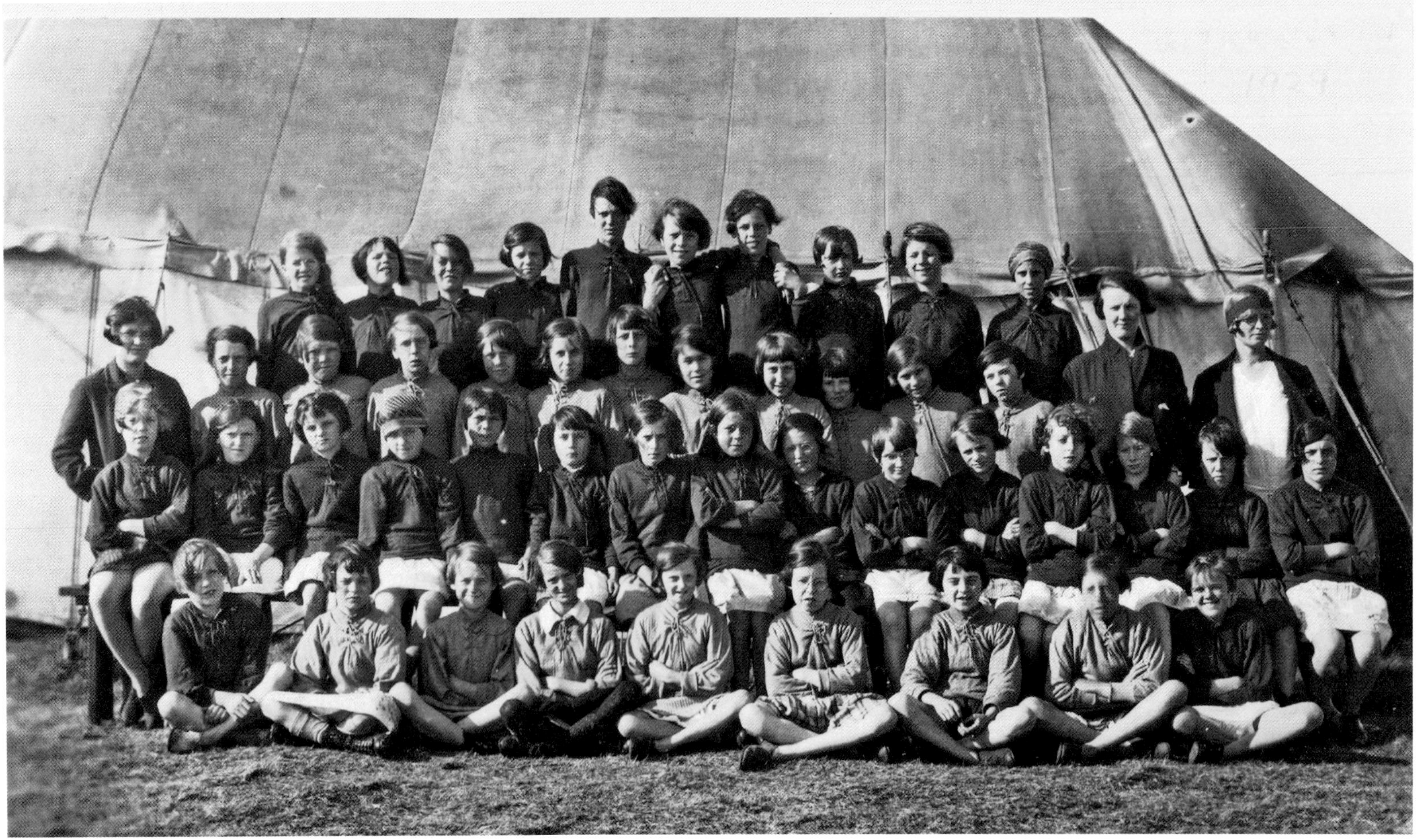

Social provision before the Welfare State was often dependent on charitable giving, with occasional state support, a hybrid arrangement that was tested in the late 1920s. Conditions in the mining industry had steadily deteriorated until, by the middle of 1927, as many as 250,000 men were out of work and only got the dole if they could prove they were looking for work in places where there was none. Along with their families one million or more people were destitute. Recognising their plight, the Lord Mayor of London, along with his counterparts in Cardiff and Newcastle (south Wales and the north east were the worst affected areas) launched an appeal for funds in April 1928. It achieved only modest success, but a re-launch in November that year concentrated minds. The government stepped in pledging a pound for every pound donated and the Prince of Wales added his voice to the appeal. It is possible that these girls benefited from the fund because a note on this picture describes it as the 'Lord Mayor of London's North East Miners' Relief Camp, Warkworth, 1929'.

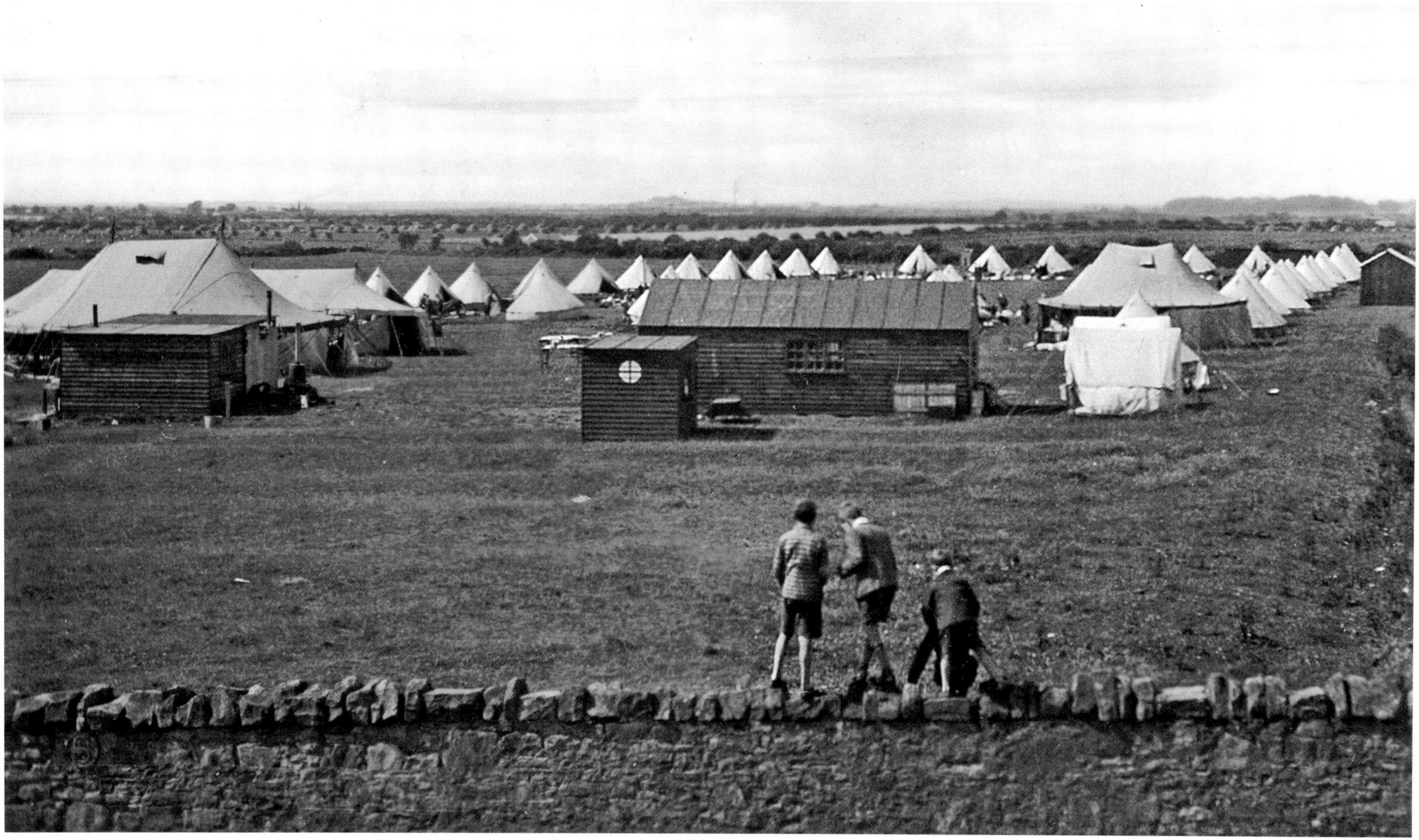

The Lord Mayor's Fund 'for the relief of the distressed mining areas' was formally closed on 30th April 1929 having raised nearly two million pounds, and it was wound up a year later, but there were other similar funds – one of which established the Lord Mayor's Holiday Camp site on the links at Amble. For four weeks spread over July and August it catered for 1,000 children from poor households, 500 boys and 500 girls in batches of 250 at a time. This picture of the camp in the early 1930s was sent as a postcard to Cleadon, near Sunderland. The message reads: 'Dear Mother, I am having a good time and eating a lot. The weather is changeable, but we are still alive'. Now, changeable weather could be expected, but 'still alive', was there something at Amble that a mother should worry about? Evidently not, the camp was regarded as good and friendly and was latterly equipped with huts. It continued to provide holidays up to the Second World War when it became Prisoner of War Camp No. 635.

Situated on the links at Birling, close to the historic mouth of the River Coquet, Warkworth Golf Course was opened in 1891. It had been designed by one of the legendary figures in the game, Old Tom Morris. A native of St. Andrews, in Scotland, he was a greenkeeper and professional who came second in the inaugural Open Championship and won it the next two years, and twice thereafter. He also designed a number of courses including Warkworth, which although of only nine holes, had eighteen tees to give the course a different challenge the second time around. The pictures show the clubhouse in the 1920s and the long, par four, second hole known, appropriately, as the 'Dunes'.

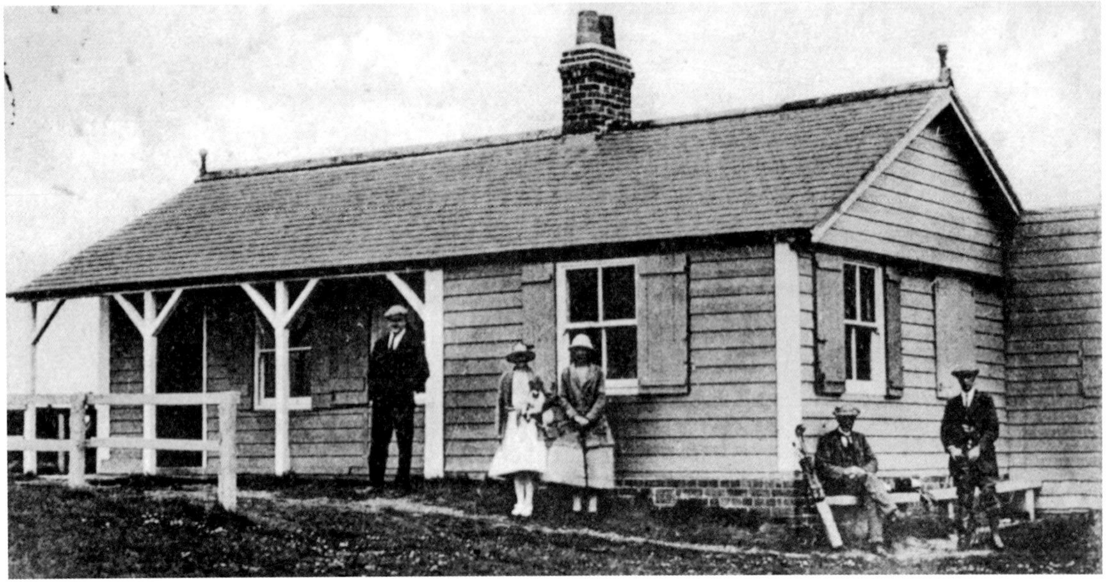

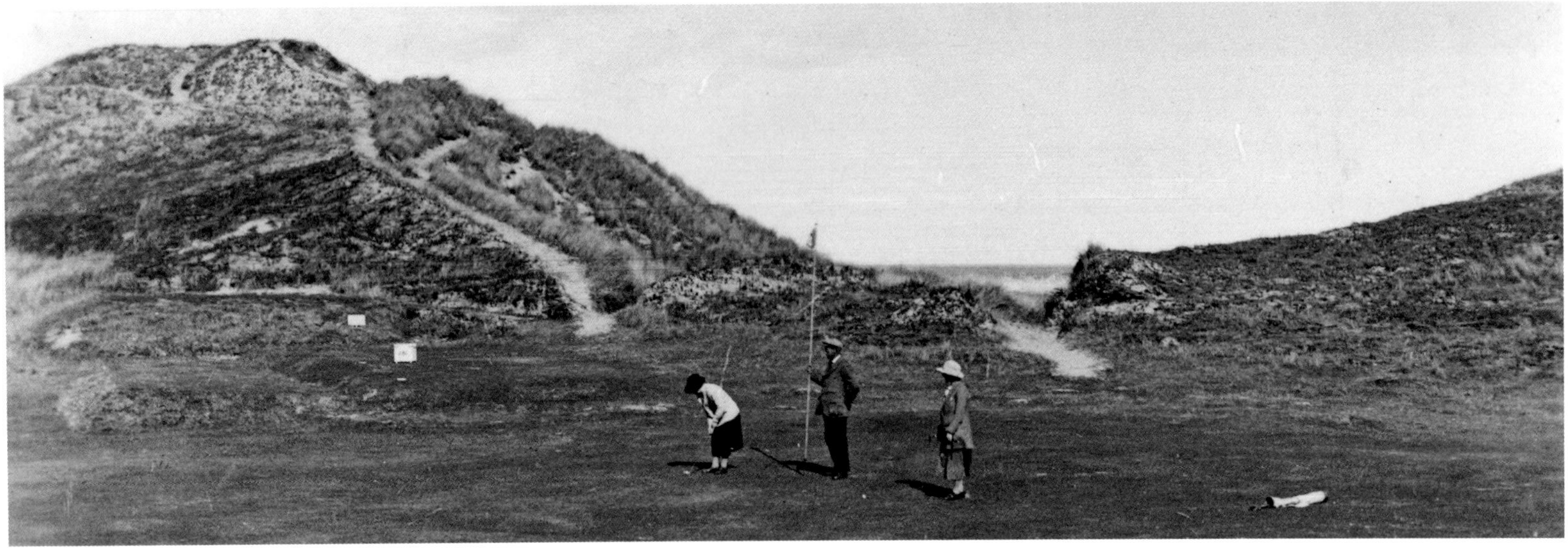